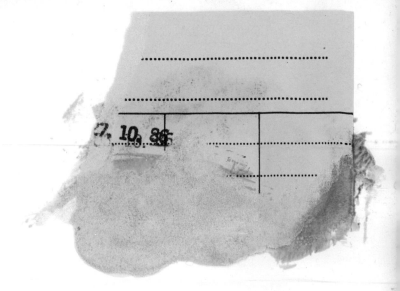

The Elephant
that Swallowed
a Nightingale

The Elephant that Swallowed a Nightingale

and other operatic wonders

CHARLES NEILSON GATTEY

Hutchinson

London Melbourne Sydney Auckland Johannesburg

Hutchinson & Co. (Publishers) Ltd
An imprint of the Hutchinson Publishing Group
17-21 Conway Street, London W1P 5HL

Hutchinson Group (Australia) Pty Ltd
30-32 Cremorne Street, Richmond South, Victoria 3121
PO Box 151, Broadway, New South Wales 2007

Hutchinson Group (NZ) Ltd
32-34 View Road, PO Box 40-086, Glenfield, Auckland

Hutchinson Group (SA) Pty Ltd
PO Box 337, Bergvlei 2012, South Africa

First published 1981
© Charles Neilson Gattey 1981

Set in Times by Bookens, Saffron Walden, Essex

Printed in Great Britain by the Anchor Press Ltd
and bound by Wm Brendon & Son Ltd
both of Tiptree, Essex
ISBN 0 09 146060 3

British Library Cataloguing in Publication Data

Gattey, Charles Neilson
    The elephant that swallowed a nightingale.
    1. Opera
    I. Title
    782.1   ML1700

    ISBN 0-09-146060-3

For Vivian Liff

Contents

Overture

'It would be difficult to conceive of a more absurd art-form than that of opera. We are asked to accept that in moments of emotion it is natural for men and women to express their deepest feelings in trills and *roulades*. We are exposed to the spectacle of ladies in the rudest of health who tenaciously postpone their dying gasp in a cascade of endless *portamenti*. We see staid and sober gentlemen suddenly break into song when we are convinced they would be more properly employed in some respectable merchant bank or counting house. Empires are destroyed in the space of an intermezzo. Villains are overthrown in the time it takes to gargle an aria. A five-minute duet is all that is needed to pledge a lifelong troth.'

JAMES HARDING
in the introduction to his biography of Massenet

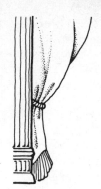
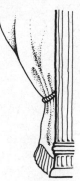

The Singing
'Venus de Kilo'

Opera, like nature, is full of wonders. Plutarch tells how a youth picked all the feathers from the scrawny body of a nightingale and then, on seeing what a tiny thing was left, exclaimed: 'Surely thou art all voice and nothing else!' Sometimes in the past when a prima donna has made her first entrance in an opera, an irreverent member of the audience may have thought: 'Surely thou art but a mountain of flesh and nothing else!'

Prima donnas have often been plagued by weight problems. It was the great mezzo-soprano Marietta Alboni (1826-94) who, beautiful in her youth, later became the stoutest singer of her times, so that Rossini, whose only pupil she was, described her as 'the elephant that swallowed a nightingale'. She had a carriage specially constructed on account of her bulk, and her appetite was such that she would often dine on two whole chickens, two large rumpsteaks, a soup tureen full of macaroni and many other titbits.

Far from being depressed by her excess kilos, Mme Alboni radiated happiness and was witty and amusing. Even when she was old, admiring artists crowded her musical *salon*. Being too stout to stand or walk, she received seated in a large armchair from where she would charm the guests with her vocal magic, watched over by her still-faithful husband.

Another soprano, Marie Wilt, was known in Vienna as the 'Imperial Elephant'. Blanche Marchesi, in *A Singer's Pilgrimage*, published in 1923, described her as having the finest voice she had ever heard, and also as being 'of exaggerated proportions, very tall and immensely fat'. Though ugly, Marie had an attractive kind smile and laughed whole-heartedly like a child. Blanche Marchesi wrote:

In operas like *Norma* or as Donna Anna, well-made and richly draped costumes could hide her figure, but her Ophelia is quite unforgettable . . . even the Viennese public, who worshipped her wonderful, unique voice could not refrain from smiling, and some even hid their faces in their hands or closed their eyes tightly from the moment she appeared on the stage.

I see her in the *Mad Scene;* the chorus girls standing on both sides instantly become pigmies by contrast. She stands there, a head taller than anyone, clad in a heavy, ungraceful white cashmere dress, her hair made up in the fashion of about 1850, crowned with an enormous wreath of what you would call seaweed, falling over her face . . . . She distributes the flowers among the girls. 'Here's rosemary, here's rue for remembrance', and as she proceeds one forgets the comic horror caused by her entrance. The sounds of matchless beauty, the perfect runs will never be heard any more, and if she had been twice as big and twice as funny, her singing would always have carried her audience away. Some people called her the hippopotamus that had swallowed a nightingale, but, curiously enough, in my remembrance the nightingale only survives, and I mention her physical defects to show how great was the power of her art.

Poor Marie Wilt fell hopelessly in love at the age of 58 with a man many years younger than herself who, on account of her corpulence, did not return her love, and she committed suicide by throwing herself out of a fourth-floor window.

A superb voice alone cannot always triumph over the handicap of an incongruous appearance. During a première of Verdi's *La traviata* at the Teatro la Fenice in Venice on 6 March 1853, when the doctor announced in the last act that Violetta, played by the inordinately fat Mme Salvini-Donatelli, had only a few hours to live, there came laughter, whistles, and a cruel spectator shouted: 'I see no consumption – I see only dropsy!' As the act continued, the laughter grew to such an extent that the music could scarcely be heard, and as a result the first night proved a complete fiasco.

Signora Visconti, known for her shrill, flexible voice, and popular in Rome in the 1730s, was so enormous that when her age was being discussed and an admirer said she was but two and twenty, Lord Chesterfield riposted: 'You mean stone, sir, not years.' And in this century Toscanini in a moment of exasperation told Zinka Milanov, who was endowed with an ample bosom: 'Oh, madam, if only those were brains, you would be the greatest soprano of all.'

The Singing 'Venus di Kilo'

It is certainly unwise for a massive prima donna and a slender one to be seen together in the same opera. Maria Malibran in 1831 appeared in Paris in the title role of Rossini's *Otello* with Wilhelmine Schroeder-Devrient as Desdemona. This proved a disaster, for, as Chopin wrote, 'It looked as if Desdemona would smother Otello.'

Some sixty-three years later Henry Abbey at the Metropolitan cast slim Marie Van Zandt as Mignon to stout Lilli Lehmann's Philine, which combination one critic compared to 'a steam locomotive drawing a horsecar'.

The hearty meals consumed by some singers were often not due to greed but to the fact that they needed these calories to build up reserves of energy. Ernestine Schumann-Heink certainly required them for the Wagnerian roles in which she excelled. A friend once saw her in a restaurant with a huge steak before her. 'Surely you aren't going to eat all that alone?' he asked. 'No, not alone,' she replied, 'with potatoes, then apple pie and cream.'

Frances Alda would breakfast on porridge, kippers, toast and jelly, followed at eleven by a dozen oysters, and she usually lunched on several platefuls of chicken stew.

Luisa Tetrazzini shared with her best friend, Caruso, a fondness for food. When in New York together, at least twice a week he would invite her to lunch in his suite at the Plaza and for dinner at Del Pezzo's or at Pane's on West 47th Street, and they would feast on Neapolitan dishes. This most lovable of prima donnas all her life refused to diet, and one evening, after a late lunch of spaghetti with Enrico, finding the pressure from her corsets unbearable, she removed them. As a result, when as Violetta she lay dying and John McCormack, playing Alfredo, raised her, he felt, to quote his words, 'as though my arms were fondling a pair of Michelin tyres'. The astonishment in his face started her laughing, in which, to the amazement of the audience, he found himself joining.

Tetrazzini had no inhibitions about her girth and enjoyed joking about it. 'I would not diet. If I diet, my face sag,' she once quipped in 1921. On the first of her many 'farewell' tours of America, she allowed the *Evening Public Ledger* in Philadelphia to publish a photograph of her with the caption 'PLUMP AND PROUD OF IT'. There followed an interview with the paper's reporter headed:

15

The Elephant that Swallowed a Nightingale

'SURE TETRAZZINI IS FAT. DOESN'T CARE WHO KNOWS IT.' The account began:

Now, listen, you ladies who wear out-sizes, and be proud of your plumpness. 'Some are born to be thin,' said Tetrazzini today, 'others to be fat. I belong to the latter class. And I am not the least ashamed of it. Why should I be? But see!' Here the soprano showed an astounding forearm. She had not exaggerated. The finest athlete in the world would have been proud to own the muscle and sinew displayed.

Luisa's favourite gown was of black sequins patterned with a huge peacock, the head of which was on her shoulders, the neck and body across her broad bosom, whilst the coloured tail stretched across her solid stern. Ivor Newton, who accompanied her at concerts in England, was always afraid of treading on this splendid train and damaging it. 'Did you ever see a train like that?' he once asked a fireman, who retorted: 'It's not the train I'm looking at – it's the engine what's pulling it!'

When Newton asked her later why she had given up singing opera, she answered: 'Because no stage carpenter is capable of building a bridge which wouldn't collapse under me!'

At least one prima donna became a voracious eater owing to matrimonial troubles. This was Mme Nordica, whose huge voice, according to Henry Finck, 'the biggest orchestra could not submerge in its tidal waves of sound', and who was deserted by husband number three after he had lost most of her money playing the stock market. As a result she had a nervous breakdown, from which she recovered through gormandizing and eventually, to quote the critic, James G. Huneker, she looked 'like a large, heavily upholstered couch'.

But one must be careful not to judge on appearances alone, for the well-fed look can be caused by the very act of singing, which makes the rib cage become larger and gives an artist a misleading air of being overweight.

The whole vexing subject has concerned some musical critics. Learning that Richard Strauss was busy completing his opera *Die Frau ohne Schatten*, a cynic among them asked: 'Where does he expect to find a prima donna able to impersonate "A Woman Without a Shadow"?'

The Singing 'Venus de Kilo'

In his *Opera Nights* Ernest Newman wrote:

I doubt whether any human being has ever heard a single perfect performance of an opera. Nature is so stupid: she has the most unfortunate gift for placing the right voice in the wrong body . . . . We get a young woman fresh from the conservatoire whose monstrous bulk suggests to the spectator only what Ysaÿe used to call the *Venus de kilo*. She looks like an ox; she moves like a cart horse; she stands like a haystack. . . . Yet because nature has seen fit to give her a vocal organ of exceptional lightness, liquidity and capacity for coloratura, she is cast, as a matter of course, for some such flower-light, gem-bright creature as Lakmé, Violetta or Rosina.

Blanche Cole, the English soprano, was a favourite with Victorian audiences following her successful début as Amina in *La sonnambula* at the Crystal Palace in 1869. Twenty years later, describing a visit to Covent Garden to hear her, Bernard Shaw in his guise of 'Corno di Bassetto', the critic of the *Star*, complained:

Madame Belle Cole's voice is less free and resonant than it was. But how is the importance of physical training for singers to be duly insisted on if critics shrink from personalities? The training of a champion wrestler, who is nothing if not eighteen stone, is one thing: the training of a vocalist is another; but both have, within certain limits, power to choose their own weight. For instance, no human being need weigh more than fourteen stone at most unless he or she pleases. I remember Tietjens as Fidelio and as Margaret; and I cannot help asking myself whether mischief such as she did to the poetry of the lyric drama for years by associating its heroines with monstrous obesity is never to be rebuked or even noticed by a suffering public. Loth as I am to condemn a lady to drink nothing for two months except six gallons of boiling water per diem, yet there are circumstances which justify this extremity. I venture desperately to blurt out to Madame Belle Cole that if she continues to grow as she has grown since the middle of the season, she will, in a few years, be quite fat. And fat spoils artists . . . . Macadam designed a little ring, through which he declared that a stone must be small enough to pass before it was fit for paving. The entrance to our concert platforms should be guarded by a hoop of standard diameter – say six feet to begin with – through which all the artists should be compelled to pass successively before taking part in the performance.

Nowadays the public expects its singing goddesses to be able to

17

slip through a hoop much less in diameter than the generous 6 feet 'Corno di Bassetto' suggested. Maria Callas in 1953 weighed some 97 kilos (15 stone), and when engaged to appear at the Metropolitan it was tactfully put to her that she must do something about this. During that summer she lost nearly half her weight, chiefly thanks to her giving up her bedtime snack of fried eggs, potatoes and cheese. Six years later an Italian manufacturer attempted to stimulate his sales of low-starch protein spaghetti by claiming in advertisements that she owed her streamlined shape to eating it. Callas brought an action against him for libel and won.

Skinniness, too, can cause problems. When Emma Calvé, the French soprano, made her début as Cherubino the page, she padded her calves beneath her tights with cotton wool in order to camouflage her lean shanks. Unfortunately, during the first act the stuffing started slipping until the backs of her legs looked as though they were sprouting potatoes. The audience began laughing, and when Calvé next appeared with all lumps removed she received a spontaneous ovation.

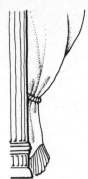
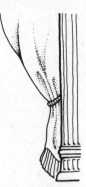

Bottled Air
from La Scala

Before beginning her career, the aspirant prima donna will usually have her voice trained. This can be a painful process for those who cannot avoid hearing her. Edward Lear complained in a letter to Lady Strachey, dated 24 January 1859: 'A vile beastly rottenheaded foolbegotten brazen-throated pernicious piggish screaming, tearing, roaring, perplexing, splitmecrackle crashmecriggle insane ass of a woman is practising howling below-stairs with a brute of a singing master so horribly, that my head is nearly off.'

Teachers of singing have often been targets for derision. As early as 1720 the Venetian composer Benedetto Marcello wrote in *Il teatro alla moda*:

The teacher will not pay any attention to rhythm, pronunciation or intonation, and he will see to it that no one in the audience will be able to understand a single word of what the vocalist is singing.

The central objective of the teaching will be the production of a few unnatural sounding tones in extremely high or low registers; thus the singer will be able to demand a correspondingly substantial increase in pay.

If the teacher should be unable to execute a trill properly himself he should not teach it to his pupils either, but tell them it is outmoded . . . .

The greatest teacher of the following century, Mme Mathilde Marchesi, wrote in *The Art of Singing* in 1862:

Every musician – amateur or instrumental professor – fancies himself capable of undertaking the production of the voice and competent to teach singing. Each one seeks to invent a new system, and each one thinks he has found the right thing. One makes his pupils sing with the mouth shut, another with the mouth wide open, a third with the mouth distorted into a kind of grin. A fourth is of the opinion that it is necessary to practise at the top of one's voice four or five hours a day, and yet a fifth says the pupil should murmur pianissimo. One professor maintains that there are no registers, another that there are as many as four or five.

One, still more ignorant than the rest, states that the chest voice is produced from the chest, and the head voice from the head. Many make their pupils sing with the head bent down, others with the body well forward, swinging to and fro. As to the emission of the voice, one teaches that the note must be given with the breath *ha* with the open glottis, while another thinks of obtaining the purity of the attack by a repeated *staccato*. Both methods are as fatiguing for the voice as they are dangerous. Others who have not the slightest notion of the stroke of the glottis, have the tone produced with *la la, da da, ga ga, na na*, etc.

And what shall I say about the many impossible theories of taking the breath? Of late it had become the fashion to breathe through the nose with the mouth tightly closed, which, if done repeatedly and quickly, produces a very unmusical sound.

She knew a teacher of singing in Vienna who used to place her finger on the larynx of her unfortunate pupils, to prevent it from moving up or down. As a result all suffered from cramp in the larynx.

Things had not improved much sixty years later, for Mme Marchesi's daughter Blanche, in *A Singer's Pilgrimage* (1923), commented even more caustically on quack singing-teachers. One claimed that he would reveal to any person coming to him for lessons 'a jealously guarded secret about voice production found in an Egyptian tomb two thousand years ago'. Another taught his pupils that cheeks must never touch teeth as this reduced sonority, and that stuffing each side of the mouth with dried prunes or chestnuts would double the sound. Blanche described as a method nothing short of a miracle that of the instructor who insisted the only way to sing was *without* the larynx.

A popular professor's former pupil told Blanche that he was made to lie down on the floor so many minutes a day, breathing slowly and deeply, whilst bricks were heaped on his chest with the aim of fortifying the muscles. He had reached a total of thirty bricks by the time he ceased having lessons.

Bottled Air from La Scala

A woman consulting Mlle Marchesi described how her first teacher had also ordered her to lie flat and in her case had put a large tumbler full of water on her chest, saying that if when she breathed it remained balanced, all was well. This performance took place at the beginning of every lesson, the rest of the time being generally spent in mopping up the water that would spill all over the pupil and the floor.

The oddest practice for a curious passer-by to watch must have been the 'dog's breath' exercise. After panting like a dog does following a sharp run, the student had to take ten deep, long breaths before the open window, run back and 'play doggie' again.

Not so amusing was what happened to the pupil who went to a Dresden teacher. He used a piece of lead to keep down the tongue. It slipped into her interior and had to be fished out. An instructor who believed in Draconian methods employed a wire cage to ensure an open mouth; costing a guinea, it was made in one size only.

Similar to this was the method of making pupils keep a sixpence edgewise between upper and lower front teeth when practising *roulades*, so as to retain the arch of the lips and the proper tone throughout in scale-singing. Persons of timid nature, fearful of swallowing the coin, used grooved ivory pencils.

In Paris there was a teacher who in the very first lesson criticized the newcomer's breathing, blaming her ill-fitting corsets, and, insisting that this must be put right at once, took her into an inner room where his *corsetière* wife proceeded to measure her for expensive new ones.

It would seem that those longing for fame were astonishingly credulous. There was a man who sold Italian water, saying: 'The voice in Italy is so good because the water is good, so if you drink plenty of it you will gain an Italian voice.' He found this a lucrative line at 5 francs a bottle. A rival teacher then started selling 'amoniaphones', which he declared were tubes containing compressed Italian air – the best in the world for the voice!

Almost forty years before Blanche Marchesi wrote of this, a Dr Moffat lecturing in Glasgow in 1884 to an audience of mostly medical men and music critics, had also recommended the air of Italy as a stimulus to singing. According to a report in the *Musical Times* for February that year, he claimed that the presence of hydrogen peroxide in the Italian air and dew contributed to the beauty of the vocal tone of singers from that country. He persuaded a number of his listeners to inhale a chemical compound made to represent Italian air. The audience was apparently impressed with the effects this had on the voices of these guinea-pigs. 'A full, clear, rich, mellow tone was produced,' states the report, which continues: 'Taking what was originally a voice of power and resonance, but destitute of intonation [sic], he showed how by chemical means this could become a tenor of great compass. Some twenty notes, ranging from the lower to the higher register, were sung without any effort by the possessor of a voice of this character.'

The next issue of the same journal carried an account of a lecture by Lennox Browne, senior surgeon at the Central Throat and Ear Hospital and also surgeon to the Royal Society of Musicians, in which he attacked Dr Moffat's theory, arguing that 'there was nothing to show that peroxide of hydrogen existed in a greater proportion in the towns and cities of Italy than elsewhere, and that on the contrary the air in most Italian towns was most insanitary'.

Coming to more recent times, Robert Merrill in his autobiography tells of a singing-teacher in New York whose studio was opposite that of his own instructor, and from the open windows of which emerged some astonishing sounds. This crank believed that women could gain most resonance by singing 'Meow!' and men could achieve the same by barking – in which they would be joined by the dogs in the vicinity. For such tuition the fee was $10 a half-hour.

For an extra charge, the stopper of a large vacuum flask would be removed for a few seconds so that a promising pupil could take a deep breath of the voice-invigorating air the professor had brought back not merely from Italy but from La Scala itself.

Also in the United States, Joan Hammond once gave a recital at a college, and afterwards its pushing young singing-master persuaded her to hear his two most promising pupils. To her surprise, she found herself expected to listen to their warming-up exercises. These astonished her. The first girl gravely took from the top of the piano a clothes-peg and fixed it on her nose, completely closing the nostrils so that no air could enter or escape. The teacher then told her to sing scales and played the chord of C major. She tried to follow him up as long as she could. Miss Hammond found it all unbearably painful. Even worse were the sounds made by the second student who stuck out her tongue and held it while attempting to sing her scales.

After half an hour of these antics, the hopefuls embarked on two songs and two arias each. One had a contralto voice of some merit, but her companion, whom the maestro introduced as 'a rich contralto', was in reality a soprano. Joan Hammond realized that the man knew next to nothing about voice production, and when she inquired the purpose of the peg and tongue practising, he stared and exclaimed: 'Surely you use one of these methods yourself?'

The great Australian singer retorted that she most certainly did not and, inwardly fuming, warned him that if he continued to train his pupils in such a cranky manner it would have disastrous consequences. 'Where did you learn to sing?' she demanded.

The other was ruffled. 'I don't sing,' he angrily admitted.

Astounded by his reply, Joan Hammond asked whether he had studied the art, and was informed that he had played for the pupil of 'one of our finest teachers' and was carrying on his methods.

The discussion came to an abrupt end with the offended fellow strutting off with music, peg and victims. There were many other further questions Miss Hammond says she would have liked to put to him, such as whether all those he taught had to use the same nose peg. The agent booking her tours revealed later that he had received an adverse report on her performance from the college, and she was never invited to return. The charlatan had his revenge.

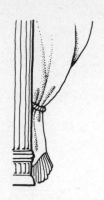
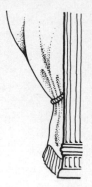

Behaving like a Prima Donna

A young soprano was once told by her mother: 'Your voice must be the principal instrument in the orchestra – that is the meaning of the words, prima donna.'

Benedetto Marcello in *Il teatro alla moda* has some amusing advice for the singer whose ambition is to become one. She should commence her career before the age of thirteen. 'It does not matter if she is unable to read. All she needs is to memorize a few familiar arias . . . which she will sing on every possible occasion. The study of solfeggio would be dangerous.'

Marcello advises that when offered her first role, the aspirant must demand the lead. If unsuccessful, she should sign the contract in any case, accepting 'a part of secondary, third, or even fourth importance'. 'The modern virtuosa', whose example should be followed, says Marcello, sings cadenzas that last for an hour each, and stops frequently to take a breath. She always attempts to sing the highest notes which are beyond her range, and during every trill she turns and twists her neck. If the conductor asks her range, she must pretend it is two or three notes above and below that which it is.

She will often attend rehearsals at other opera-houses. During these she should start applauding a singer when everyone else is silent, like that no one can fail to notice her presence. Then she should turn to a neighbour and declare: 'Why is it that they never give such an aria to me? . . . Just listen how that wonderful creature who is paid a fortune in lire manages to muffle every single, effective note!'

A prima donna should ignore the *seconda donna*, Marcello stresses, so should the *seconda* the *terza*, and so on. If they are on the stage together, they must never listen to one another, and while one sings an aria the other should join her 'protector' standing in the wings, accept some snuff from him and blow her nose loudly.

The modern virtuosa will endeavour to sing her arias differently every night though her variations may result in harsh dissonances with the bass or the violins whether the latter double her part or have an independent accompaniment. If she should start singing in the wrong key – this will be of no importance either as all modern conductors are tone-deaf. Whenever the virtuosa has exhausted her supply of variations she might try to insert embellishments even in the trills. This is about the only thing which the virtuosas of the present time have not tried yet.

When singing duets, according to Marcello, the vocalist ought never to rehearse with her partner, and especially during the cadenza she should take all the time she wants to show off her long trills. The best way for her to depict emotion is by rolling her eyes, distorting her features and toying with a beautiful handkerchief, which should be brought to her on the stage by a page.

Whenever in an aria, 'cruel', 'traitor', 'tyrant', and similar words occur she will smile at her rich protector. When uttering such words as 'dearest', 'my own' or 'my life' she will turn towards the prompter, the bear, or some extra. She will shed torrential tears (because of professional jealousy) whenever there is applause for any other singer, or for the bear, or for stage effects such as an earthquake.

The virtuosa should know by heart everyone else's part better than her own and sing it with them during the performance. If her 'protector' should talk to or applaud some young girl, she will scold him violently, saying: 'Stop this nonsense at once – or shall I box your ears or slap your face, you deceitful old idiot?'

Marcello ends his advice by saying that when the finale is reached and the other characters are singing or speaking, the virtuosa must ignore them and do all she can to attract the attention of the audience to herself.

The Venetian satirist might have added that to behave like the legendary prima donna it is important to know better than anybody else on every subject. In the case of Lilli Lehmann this included interpreting the mysteries of railroad timetables. Once, in

America's Wild West, she insisted on leaving a train at a lonely halt to catch a connection, and called the conductor an ass when he tried to stop her. But he was right, for no train appeared and she was stranded for two days.

The only subject a true prima donna ought to treat as unworthy of her serious attention is income tax. Birgit Nilsson once asked one of the accountants at the Metropolitan to help her fill in the forms she had received. Her reply to the question 'Have you any dependants?' was 'Yes – impresario Rudolf Bing'.

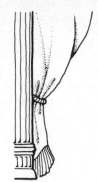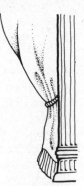

Mr Prima Donna

Asked what dependants she had, another Queen of Song might have replied, 'My consort'. Henry Sutherland Edwards, the discerning music critic of the now defunct *St. James's Gazette*, wrote amusingly in the 1890s about the role of the prima donna's husband. Praise to her being as necessary as water to a hydrangea, on arrival in any important town where she was to sing, almost his first duty should be to discover who were the most influential critics, which of them could with advantage to her be cultivated, and 'which by reason of notorious surliness or some other similar defect had better be left alone'.

When a prima donna's début at an opera house had been fixed, it was for her husband to arrange the presentation of the bouquets, the wreaths and the garland; to supervise the recalls; to see that the carriage in which she had intended to drive home was unhorsed so that it would be drawn by her admirers; and towards the end of the season to see that she received a 'spontaneous' gift of a set of diamonds from the subscribers. These manifestations of delight must, of course, be varied according to the custom of the country in which she was singing, for what would in one land arouse enthusiasm might in another provoke laughter.

'A flight of doves, for instance, each dove bearing a streamer with a sonnet inscribed on it, might be very effective in England. In Russia, after a great success a prima donna is seldom recalled less than a dozen times, but this in England would be simply tiresome'. Bouquets, however, might be thrown on to the stage in London opera houses in profusion, and it was for the husband to see that the supply was adequate to the occasion.

Some husbands took their wives' place at rehearsals, and not only paid visits in their names but also received at home in lieu of them. Edwards continued:

One husband is reported to have carried this species of infatuation so far as to offer to sit for his wife's portrait. But even the most modest of husbands will, in speaking of his wife's engagements and performances, say 'we' when he ought to say 'she'. 'We have now thirty characters in our repertoire.'; 'We are getting up the part of Flora.'; 'We had a great success last night.': these are phrases continually in the mouth of every prima donna's husband.

Other husbands lived upon their wives' earnings and, too proud to perform the duties of shawl-bearer, made a point of never being seen in public with them. 'Sometimes the prima donna's singing-master, recognizing her talent beforehand, snaps her up . . . . Or if she has escaped her singing-master, the manager is probably lying in wait for her with an engagement not for a stipulated number of years but for life.'

Michael Kelly in his *Reminiscences* says that Félican, Elizabeth Billington's second husband, was 'deeply in love with her English guineas' which she earned for singing at Covent Garden. The manager of that opera house once complained to Angelica Catalani's husband that the high fees he extorted on her behalf made it impossible to engage other fine singers. 'Does that matter?' retorted M. Valabrèque. 'My wife and a few puppets are quite sufficient for any theatre.' He knew so little about music that when Angelica complained a piano was too high, he had 2 inches sawn off its legs.

In this century, too, managers have sometimes been at odds with husbands. Giovanni Battista Meneghini used to insist on collecting in cash after every performance the fee due to his wife, Maria Callas, for singing in the USA. This annoyed Rudolf Bing at the Metropolitan, so he gave him more to carry away by paying over the money in $1 bills. When another star's husband brought back the contract his wife had already signed to argue over a clause and try to squeeze some extra money out of Gatti-Casazza, the latter took the document, cut off his signature and handed back the worthless paper.

A few husbands are free from interest in business matters and want to lead a quiet life. Gerald Moore in his *Farewell Recital* wrote with admiration of Victoria de los Angeles, whom he had often accompanied at the piano. This happy relationship had been clouded only by the fact that her husband, Enrique Magriña, believed in *mañana* and employed a secretary to destroy all correspondence unopened. According to Moore, no one to his knowledge had received a letter from Magriña and in all the time he played for this soprano he never managed to obtain details of a programme he was anxious to practise until a few days before the recital.

It is, of course, the duty of the perfect husband to applaud his wife. Berlioz in his *Evenings with the Orchestra* said they are of more value than lovers, who usually dread ridicule and also secretly fear that too great a success for the prima donna will add to their rivals.

A well-trained husband, Berlioz suggested, should have 'the gifts of ventriloquism and vocal disguise'. He might begin his own performance in the balcony with shouts of '*Brava!*' in the chest-notes of a tenor; from there he dashes to the corridor behind the first row of boxes, thrusting his head momentarily through the openings in the doors whilst booming in a deep bass voice: 'Admirable!', etc. Then he pants up the stairs to the third tier where he makes the house ring with his 'Delightful! Exquisite! Ye Gods, what a talent!' – all uttered in feminine tones choked with emotion.

There you have the model husband, hard-working and intelligent. As for the one who is a man of taste, who remains quietly in his seat during an entire act, and who considers it bad form ever to applaud his own wife, it may be said of him: 'As a husband he is lost, unless his wife is an angel of fidelity.'

Berlioz wondered whether a husband invented the 'hissing success'. If the public hears a prima donna too often during a season, it can begin to take her for granted and applaud insufficiently for her liking. To put this right, a loyal but little-known friend is given a seat in a dark corner. According to Berlioz:

Just as the diva gives unmistakable proof of her talent, he starts to hiss as stridently and insultingly as possible. The whole house rises in indignation and a deafening storm of avenging plaudits bursts out. But so audacious a ruse requires skilful handling – besides there are very few women prepared to submit to the affront of a feigned hiss, whatever the subsequent rewards may prove to be.

In fact, Berlioz adds: 'I am sure there are artistes who are childish enough when travelling by rail to weep and suffer a thousand torments every time the engine whistles.'

Rudolf Bing in real life did what Berlioz suggested in jest. Following his sensational cancellation of Callas's contract to sing at the Metropolitan in 1958, the manager feared there would be a hostile reception when Leonie Rysanek appeared instead as Lady Macbeth in Verdi's opera, so he hired a claqueur to shout 'We want Callas!' the moment Leonie first came on to the stage, instructing him to do this from such a position that she could not catch his words. Being a shrewd psychologist, Bing had correctly foreseen that such behaviour would rouse an American audience's sympathy for the underdog and thus he prevented those who longed to hear Callas sing the role from voicing their feelings.

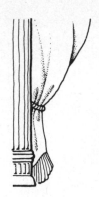
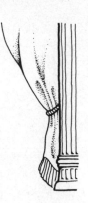

How to Breed Nightingales

Many a prima donna's husband must long for a daughter who will have a voice as glorious as her mother's, but unfortunately this has rarely happened. 'Will science ever be able to produce the kind of voice it wants, and in the numbers it would like, by intelligent breeding?' asked Ernest Newman in *The Sunday Times* of 5 September 1937. He then quoted from a book by Champfleury, who, in his *Souvenirs et Portraits de Jeunesse*, published in 1872, told of a dabbler in genetics, M. Bernard Moulin, who contended that 'children are physically, morally and intellectually living photographs of their parents taken at the moment of conception'. For the offspring of a diva, for example, to inherit her mother's vocal genius, the latter might try singing a sustained high C with ease and *bravura* whilst enjoying the ecstasies of sexual intercourse. Of course, she would have to take care to marry a music-lover.

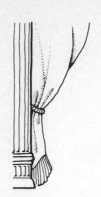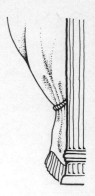

Singing and Sex

The sexiest role in opera is probably that of Don Giovanni, for, as his servant Leporello reveals to Donna Elvira, reading from a long list of names and addresses, he has had amorous adventures with 90 women in France, more than 200 in Germany, 640 in Italy, 1,003 in Spain, but only the same number in Turkey as in France – no doubt because the seraglios were so well guarded. Country girls in plenty, ladies' maids and would-be ladies, nobility and gentry, handsome, ugly, high or humble, all are women for the Don. In December, plump he'll have them; in July, he prefers them slender; and his favourite form of sinning is with one who's just beginning. But the last thing the baritone playing the part is likely to attempt is to emulate Giovanni, for he knows overdoing sex would have adverse effects on his voice.

For a tenor it can be far more dangerous. Women are generally attracted to tenors, but on winning them as husbands or lovers they often discover that many – especially the Latins – avoid intercourse for several days before a performance, on the grounds that it can harm their high notes.

Such enforced continence can cause trouble. For example, Mario del Monaco's wife attacked Rudolf Bing in his office at the Metropolitan, accusing him of ruining her married life because he was making her husband sing so often every week.

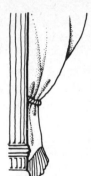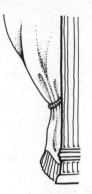

Writing and Staging
an Opera

Enough for a while of singers. The opera itself is what really matters. How do composers obtain inspiration? According to tradition, many successful ones have found that certain rites helped them to get into touch with their muse. Those hoping to emulate them might experiment to see whether any of these practices prove effective today.

It is said that Beethoven would run about bareheaded, dousing himself with cold water, whilst before Rossini put pen to paper he needed a glass of champagne. Gluck, however, would have a bottle of it on either side of him when he sat at his piano – not indoors but in the middle of his favourite meadow, thus no doubt imagining he was in the Elysian Fields when immersed in writing his *Orfeo ed Euridice*. As for Haydn, he could neither compose nor extemporize unless he wore the diamond ring Frederick the Great had given him

Sacchini, idle and dissolute, needed the close company of a beautiful woman before inspiration came. His contemporary Paisiello was only able to work when between warm sheets and yet managed to compose over a hundred operas, including *Il barbiere di Siviglia*, which used the same text as Rossini's version and was eventually eclipsed by it. Paisiello's rival, Cimarosa, specialized in comic operas, of which the best-known is *Il matrimonio segreto*. He wrote best when surrounded by a happy, chattering crowd of friends, which explains perhaps why his music is so lively and good-humoured.

Sarti pulled heavy curtains over all windows to make his study as dark as possible before settling down to compose, with a single taper for illumination; whilst Zingarelli was so devout that he would kneel and read from his missal seeking heavenly guidance, with the result that apart from operas he wrote over thirty Masses.

Anfossi, on the other hand, composed best in the kitchen, his muse being particularly stimulated by the aroma of roasting fowls and the fragrance of Bologna sausages. He produced some seventy operas which, being very light, have not endured as well as the food which inspired them.

Most meticulous of all was Cherubini, regarded by Beethoven as the greatest living composer, apart from himself, of that era. If he made a blot, he would carefully cut it out and stick a clean piece of paper over the hole, so that some of his manuscripts had a mosaic-like appearance. He not only wrote his own music but also copied out that by various Italians, filling eighteen volumes, some of which number over four hundred pages.

When seeking advice on how to write an opera, who better to consult than Benedetto Marcello? The tongue-in-cheek subtitle of his book *Il teatro alla moda* begins: 'A sure and easy method to compose well and to produce Italian operas in the modern fashion, containing useful and necessary instructions for librettists, composers . . . .'

Marcello advises the librettist to write verse by verse without any preconceived plan, for if the audience never understands the plot, their attention will be assured. The talents of the performers do not concern him, and all he need ascertain is that the impresario can readily obtain 'a good bear or lion, good thunderbolts, earthquakes, tempests, etc.'.

According to Marcello, realism is imparted to an opera by the introduction of prisons, daggers, poison, the writing of letters on the stage, wild bull hunts, murders and mad scenes. If it should be possible to introduce a scene in which the principal characters sit down and nod off while an attempt is made on their lives (which they conveniently thwart by waking up in time), then the librettist will have created something of real distinction never before seen on the Italian stage.

The librettist must have at hand a good supply of old operas (by some other writers) from which he will borrow the plot as well as the stage sets. All he has to change is the metre and the names of the characters. He can achieve similar results by translating plays from the French, by changing prose to verse, or tragedies into comedies, adding or omitting characters according to the wishes of the impresario . . . .

One rule of major importance is never to let a character exit before he has sung the usual *canzonetta*. This is especially appropriate if it immediately precedes that person's execution, suicide, or taking of poison without knowing it.

Arias, continues Marcello, must in no way be related to the preceding recitative but should be full of references to sweet little butterflies, bouquets, nightingales, little boats, rustic dwellings, jasmine, violets, tigers, lions, whales, crabs, turkeys, cold chicken and the like. In this fashion the librettist will demonstrate to everybody his aptitude as a natural scientist, who by his well-selected similes, shows off his knowledge.

Before the first night, the librettist should extol the music, the singers, the impresario, the orchestra, and the extras. Then, if the opera fails, he should blame it on the singers' inability to do justice to his intentions and on their thinking only about their notes. He should attack the composer for not understanding the dramatic strength of the scenes and concentrating only on his arias, accuse the impresario of spending too little on the scenery and properties, and claim the orchestra players and extras were continually drunk.

If the plot should require husband and wife to be imprisoned together, and if one of them should have to die, it is essential to let the other remain alive so that he or she can sing a merry aria. This will cheer up the audience as it will make them realize that the opera is only make-believe, after all.

If a letter is to be written, the writing table and a chair should be carried on to the stage by extras and be removed immediately the letter is completed. 'In royal palaces he should provide for a ballet of the gardeners and in the country for a dance of the courtiers.'

If the singers pronounce their words indistinctly, the librettist must never correct them, for clarity might impair sales to the public of the printed libretto.

The librettist should pay frequent social calls on the prima donna, since the success or failure of the opera usually depends on her. He should find out whether what he has written is worthy of her genius and make any necessary changes, lengthening or shortening her role accordingly. But he must not bore her by describing the plot.

Marcello next advises the composer in similar fashion and begins by saying that he need know nothing of the rules of good composition.

He will have little facility in reading and therefore will not make out the meaning of the speeches. If he plays the harpsichord, he will not observe the special qualities of the stringed or the wind instruments, and if he is a player of stringed instruments, he will not take pains to understand the harpsichord, being convinced that he can become a good composer in the modern manner without practical acquaintance with that instrument.

Marcello explains how it would be an advantage to the composer if he had been the copyist of some established composer and had retained the original manuscripts of the latter's operas, stealing from them ideas for arias, recitatives and choruses. Having stressed to the librettist the importance of the manuscript's being carefully punctuated, he will never read the entire opera to avoid getting confused, but will set it line by line, showing no regard for full stops, question marks, or commas.

It is of particular importance that the composer should allot the best arias to the prima donna, adapting for this purpose old forgotten ones by foreign composers. Should he be the virtuosa's teacher, he must urge her to pronounce everything indistinctly, teaching her many flashy ornaments and rapid passages for that purpose. Thus no one will understand a word, and the music will stand out better. He must also never forget that happy and sad arias should alternate throughout the opera regardless of any relevance to the text or stage action. Many should be so long that it will prove impossible for the audience to remember the opening bars by the time the middle has been reached.

The modern composer must insist that the impresario engages a large orchestra with violins, oboes, horns, and other instruments. He might spare him the expense of double-bass players, however, since he has no use for them except for tuning up before the opera starts.

The composer must assure everyone that any success was due to the prima donna's genius. This he should say, out of her hearing, to all the other singers in turn, to everyone in the orchestra, and to those who arranged the earthquake, etc.

Any aria that does not succeed or become popular he will call a masterpiece ruined by the singers and beyond the limited musical taste of the audience.

Finally, the composer will have the following printed prominently immediately after the cast list: 'The music is by the most renowned of all composers, the celebrated Signor . . . , conductor of the orchestra, of concerts, of chamber concerts, dancing-master, fencing-master, etc., etc., etc.'

Libretto and score completed, the next step to a production is for the impresario to engage a scenic designer who, Marcello says, ought to know nothing about perspective, architecture or lighting. He should design sets as if viewed from four or six different points at the same time, with the horizon assumed to be at a different level for each. This kind of variety would please the eyes of spectators immensely.

The rich draperies for indoor scenes could also be used to hang across gaps in outdoor ones to protect the singers from the risk of catching cold in the open air. The horizon should always be assumed very near in order to reduce the amount of stage space to be lit. Halls, prisons, small rooms and the like need not have any door or windows. The singers will climb on to the stage directly out of the boxes in any case. Since they will have learnt at rehearsals their moves, there is no need at all to light the set.

In outdoor scenes, when one of the chief characters is supposed to fall asleep, a moss-covered settee should be carried on when required by pages or courtiers, so that the famous singer may sit and enjoy a nap while the others sing.

The lighting of the centre of the stage is of no importance and far more care should be taken over the lighting in the wings and backstage. And though the sky ought to be lighter than anything else, no one in the audience will be surprised to see a set with the properties brightly lit while the sky above is pitch black. It will be appreciated that to light the sky as well would be prohibitively expensive.

If a throne should be required on the set, it can be quickly assembled by using three steps, a chair and a canopy, but the latter is required only if the prima donna is to sit under it.

The modern scene painter must take care to employ stronger colours on properties or decorations towards the rear of the stage. This is necessary since he must distinguish himself from the outmoded methods of his predecessors who used softer shades the further the distance from the audience to create the illusion of space. But today's ambitious scenic artist who wants to make a name for himself must strive to achieve the opposite effect.

Modern stage technicians and painters must surpass themselves when it comes to preparing the set for the finale. This will receive the most applause since it will be judged by the crowds from the street, who by this time will have been let into the theatre without having to pay for admission and who in return are expected to act like a claque. It will be exceedingly effective to have a palace lowered out of the sky, beautifully illuminated and swarming with extras, who represent deities of both sexes carrying various objects symbolizing their divinity.

As soon as the opera is over, it will be the duty of those gods and goddesses, for understandable reasons of thrift, to blow out the candles on the stage and in the auditorium.

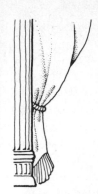
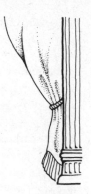

The Impresario

Far more important than anybody else, wrote Benedetto Marcello in *Il teatro alla moda*, is the impresario. He added that to be modern in 1720 the impresario should know nothing about the theatre, music, poetry or painting, should urge the librettist to write scenes that would stun the audience, must be sure to employ the bear at the end of each act, and should close the opera with the usual wedding scene or with the finding, at long last, of a missing heir or similar person whose identity may be proved through the aid of oracles, a star on his chest, a band around his ankle, or moles on his knees, tongue and ears.

Marcello states that the part of the son should always be given to a virtuoso who is twenty years older than the mother and if two important singers compete for the lead, the impresario must order the librettist to write two such roles, each of which has the same number of arias, recitatives, etc. Even the names of both characters ought to contain the same number of letters.

When he pays the bass- and the cello-players after the performance, the impresario should make deductions for the *da capo* sections of all the arias, in the course of which they had rests. With this in mind, he should approach the composer and ask him to compose these without a single bass note. Singers who had colds or who missed their cues should be paid with counterfeit coins.

During those performances for which few tickets are sold, the impresario will permit the singers to skip half their arias and to leave out the recitatives, and tell the string-players not to waste any rosin on their bows, the bear to take the evening off, and the extras to have a smoke with the principal character.

And if the opera calls for a pregnant queen or empress, the impresario should engage a virtuosa who is expecting.

Thus jested Benedetto Marcello, basing his banter no doubt on personal experience as a composer. Curiously enough, the next century's greatest diva, Patti, was born just after her mother had been playing the title role in the last act of *Norma* in Madrid's Royal Opera House.

An impresario of Victorian times deserving such pillorying would have been Léon Carvalho, who directed the Théâtre-Lyrique in Paris. He and his prima donna wife ruthlessly altered the operas which he presented and in which she appeared. James Harding wrote in his life of Gounod:

She lived in an atmosphere of adulation created by the fans who worshipped her undoubted talent as a singer. This she believed gave her the right to titivate music written by composers who had not made sufficient allowance for her genius. She loaded their melodic lines with arabesques and trills. No aria was safe from her greedy hands. Regardless of the dramatic context she gilded and gilded with majestic unconcern the music put before her. . . . Each alteration was sanctioned by the unanswerable comment: 'Variante de Mme. Carvalho'.

With supreme lack of tact, M. Carvalho would inform composers: 'Your work will be performed as though you were already dead.'

Another composer, Saint-Saëns, retaliated. He was a brilliant mimic, and in great demand at parties was his imitation of Mme Carvalho as Marguerite in Gounod's *Faust*. Wearing a blond wig with long plaits which clashed incongruously with his black beard and large nose, he would sing in a falsetto all the trills and cadenzas adorning the passage where Marguerite sits as the spinning-wheel, reproducing with astonishing accuracy the slightly off-pitch tone that Mme Carvalho, now vocally in decline, was inclined to produce.

Coming to impresarios of more recent vintage, Harold Fielding on at least one occasion has proved himself a match for any prima donna. Ivor Newton was Grace Moore's accompanist during a concert tour of Britain, and in his reminiscences, *At the Piano*, he relates how annoyed she was on arriving at the Opera House,

Blackpool, to find that her car could not be parked outside the stage door because a large Rolls-Royce had been left there. It belonged to Harold Fielding, the impresario presenting her tour. The offending vehicle had to be removed so that her own could take its place before she would alight.

When, later, Fielding visited Miss Moore in her dressing-room, she complained not only about his Rolls but also about other instances of *lèse-majesté*. 'I must remind you, Mr Fielding, that you were not at the airport to meet me, and, though this is the sixth concert of our tour, this is the first time that I have seen you.'

Harold Fielding realized that she regarded him as her servant and that he must fight back, so with an untroubled smile he informed her: 'Oh, I'm afraid I'm a prima donna impresario.'

Grace Moore's response was as cool and calm. 'Perhaps I should impress upon you, Mr Fielding, that it takes many rare gifts and a great deal of character to be a prima donna.'

Ivor Newton writes that so far as he remembers the two never met again.

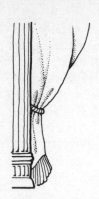
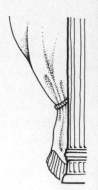

Are Rehearsals
Really Necessary?

In the nineteenth century and even in this, opera stars have often refused to attend rehearsals. Patti insisted on a clause being inserted in her contract giving her the right not to attend any, and she would send her personal maid to stand in for her instead. As a result she often did not meet the other singers performing in the same opera till the first night. Once, according to Mapleson, when *Il trovatore* was being presented, the baritone asked if he might have the honour of an introduction to Mme Patti at the very moment when he was singing in the trio of the first act. The impresario continued: 'The Manrico of the evening was exceedingly polite and managed without scandalizing the audience to effect the introduction by singing it as if it were a portion of his role.' He added that in the three or four years that Patti was with him in America she never appeared at a rehearsal.

That brilliant producer Dennis Arundell tells a story about a talented young singer who had been engaged to make her first appearance with an opera company and was asked whether she intended to have some stage coaching. 'There's no need,' she replied. 'I am *singing*.' He also relates how the bass-playing Mephistopheles in *Faust* insisted at rehearsals that throughout his career he had always crossed left on a certain line, to which Arundell retorted that if he insisted on doing so in this production he would get his teeth kicked in by the dancers.

Robert Merrill recalls that soon after joining the Metropolitan he was chosen to play Ashton to Lily Pons's Lucia. To his astonishment neither did she attend the rehearsals nor did she meet him. Then on the first night, after the opening scene in which Lucia does not appear, he had no sooner left the stage than an assistant stage manager hurried him to the diva's dressing-room, saying that she wanted to see him urgently.

Wearing a Chinese dressing-gown of silver brocade, and with four Persian cats grouped elegantly around her, Miss Pons extended a hand and no sooner had Merrill shaken it than he realized she had expected him to kiss it. 'You may wonder why I asked you to visit me today,' she began. It was to explain that acting with her was extremely simple. All he had to remember was that on the stage she would move towards him and he never towards her. Like that, each always knew where the other was. Most important of all, when in the second act she fainted, he must hurry up to her with a chair so that she might fall on to it. Did he understand? He did, so she dismissed him, saying: 'Very good. Until we meet on the stage.'

Merrill comments that their distant duels came off perfectly. 'And even when we embraced I knew I was somewhere in the same city with the great star.'

This desire to have almost the entire stage to herself has affected other divas. Grace Bumbry has been called by Gobbi 'the most distant Tosca I ever partnered'. He says that she behaved as though he was not there in the second act. She kept so far away from him that when he was supposed to sing in Italian 'Sit here', he altered this to 'Sit there'.

Many stories have been told of Sir Thomas Beecham's *badinage* at rehearsals. In 1924 during a rehearsal at His Majesty's Theatre of *Die Meistersinger*, he asked the clumsy young tenor playing Werther: 'Do you consider yours a suitable way of making love to Eva?'

'Well, there are different ways of making love,' parried the man.

'Observing your grave, deliberate motions,' returned Sir Thomas, 'I was reminded of that estimable quadruped, the hedgehog.'

After another rehearsal, this time of *Die Walküre*, he remarked afterwards of the soprano singing Brünnhilde that she reminded him of a cart coming downhill with the brakes on. And of a baritone in *Carmen*: 'He thinks he is the bull instead of the toreador.'

Sir Thomas had happier rehearsals with Conchita Supervia. On agreeing to sing for him at Covent Garden, she stipulated that her six performances in *La cenerentola* should precede her appearance in *Carmen* because, she claimed, the low *tessitura* of Bizet's opera would make it hard for her to sing Rossini's relatively high *coloratura*.

But Beecham had made up his mind to start his season with an opera that was a favourite of the public, rather than with one not produced in London for almost a century, and his decision was supported by the fact that Carmen was a role in which Supervia excelled. She, however, would not give way and went off to film in *Evensong* instead.

Later, however, the pair were reconciled and it was settled that Supervia should sing in *La cenerentola* on two evenings at the end of the season. Sir Thomas, so as to add to the visual appeal of his production, had arranged for her to travel to the ball in Cinderella tradition sitting in a crystal coach to which were harnessed six ponies. He chose a little-known Rossini overture to be played as she was drawn round the stage, and in order to time this it looked as if the animals would have to be brought to a rehearsal.

But the Spanish prima donna thought it unnecessary to go to so much trouble. 'Sir Thomas,' she called, 'and you, Geoffrey – come and be my snow-white ponies!'

No one could resist the *joie de vivre* that emanated from Conchita Supervia, and the dictatorial conductor and Geoffrey Toye, the general manager of the Royal Opera House, sprang forward without a second's hesitation, and with the diva sportively cracking a whip about their heads, the pair pranced round the stage with knees well raised amusingly imitating horses of *haute école*.

Ivor Newton, who accompanied Conchita Supervia at the piano, has written that once the rehearsal was over she told him gleefully: 'Did you see that? After all the unhappiness they caused me over this production, I got them where I wanted them. I can't tell you how I enjoyed using that whip.'

Sir Thomas himself was once reported as saying:

In spite of our little difficulties, we are really a very happy family at Covent Garden. We always meet in the morning on the best of terms. By two o'clock in the afternoon we are ready to cut each other's throats. By the middle of the evening performance ancient friendships have been broken and family ties sundered, and at the end of the day, people part, never to meet again. But at ten o'clock the next morning all is forgiven, and we start our daily round once more. That, I am sure you will agree, is the ideal state of things. How can you compare it with the flat level of monotonous existence? Happiness is impossible without continual bickering and friction. Such things are vital to human happiness.

There was one constant cause for complaint among the members of the orchestra and that was the length of the rehearsals. They led to Paul Beard, the leader of the London Philharmonic, resigning to join the BBC Symphony. He told its conductor, Sir Adrian Boult: 'I felt that just one more Wagner day at Covent Garden, ten in the morning till midnight, would be the end of me.'

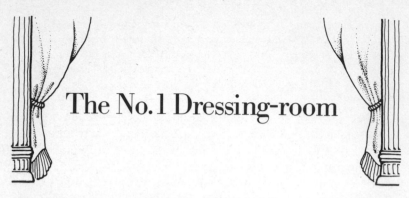

The No. 1 Dressing-room

The right not to attend rehearsals was only one of the many privileges divas used to exact from impresarios. Most coveted of all was the right to occupy the No. 1 dressing-room when singing in all the great opera houses, for having gained this a diva could regard herself as *prima donna assoluta* – absolute first lady. During her long reign at Covent Garden, Dame Nellie Melba had her own dressing-room which was kept locked, and no one else was allowed to use it when she was singing elsewhere. It had a notice fixed on the door bearing the command: 'MELBA! SILENCE! SILENCE!' When she was within, all the stage-hands had to wear rubber-soled shoes so that noisy footsteps would not disturb her, and smoking was strictly forbidden.

The opera house of Chicago in 1878 had two principal dressing-rooms, identically furnished and on either side of the stage. Etelka Gerster was regarded as the leading member of the company Colonel Mapleson had assembled for his first American tour, and she chose the one on the right for herself. The day after her performance she left to fulfil another engagement, and that evening Marie Roze, the French soprano, and Minnie Hauk were to appear as Susanna and Cherubino respectively in *The Marriage of Figaro*.

Minnie (originally Mignon Hauck) as a child had named all her cats 'Jenny Lind' and was dubbed later 'The Singing Hawk'. She was known for slapping the faces of those she disliked, so it is not surprising that when she first sang in London, in 1878, Hermann Klein, the critic, found her voice 'not remarkable for sweetness and sympathetic charm, though strong and full enough in the medium register, but somehow its rather thin, penetrating timbre sounded just right in a character whose music called for the expressing of heartless sensuality, caprice, cruelty and fatalistic defiance.' In order to secure what Gerster's choice had given the status of prima donna's dressing-room, Minnie hurried there with her maid early in the afternoon and installed her costumes and theatrical trunk in it.

Marie Roze also felt that the coveted room ought to be hers, and sent her maid at four o'clock for the purpose. On discovering that Minnie had already moved in, the servant consulted Monsieur Roze, who, assisted by stage-hands, transferred all Minnie's things to the dressing-room on the opposite side and then brought in his wife's. This accomplished, he returned to the hotel where they were staying and advised her to be in the disputed room by six o'clock in case of trouble.

Meanwhile, towards half-past five, Minnie Hauk's agent visited the opera house and, finding Mme Roze's belongings where his client's should have been, he ordered their removal, replaced Minnie's and made fast the door with a padlock before departing.

Then at six Marie arrived and, on discovering what had been done, sent for a locksmith who opened the door, and once more Minnie's possessions were ejected and the other's restored, after which Marie proceeded to change into costume.

Half an hour later, believing the desired dressing-room to be securely padlocked, Minnie made her leisurely way to the theatre. She was so enraged when faced with final defeat that she stormed out, shouting that never would she sing there again. When Mapleson learned this, he rushed to Minnie's hotel and implored her to relent, but she would not and the opera had to begin without her. The impresario had sent urgently for his lawyers, and thanks to threats of huge damages for breach of contract and the stressing of what disappointment she was causing her admirers, Minnie at last dressed herself as Cherubino and took over from her understudy half-way through *The Marriage of Figaro*.

The press made front-page news of the incident, and 'The Great Dressing-Room Disturbance', as the headlines proclaimed it, became the talk of America.

Though she lost the battle for superior accommodation, Minnie later could boast that she had risen higher than Mme Roze in the

social scale, for she married Baron Ernst von Hesse-Wartegg and
settled in the Lucerne house once occupied by Wagner.

At the old Metropolitan the star soprano would be allotted
dressing-room No. 10. On one gala occasion the programme
consisted of one act from *La traviata* with Joan Sutherland as
Violetta, one from *La Bohème* with Renata Tebaldi as Mimì, and
one from *Der Rosenkavalier* with Lisa della Casa as Octavian and
Elisabeth Schwarzkopf as the Marschallin. With admirable
diplomacy, Sir Rudolf Bing persuaded Tebaldi to accept the
second soprano's dressing-room on the grounds that as Mimì she
would be wearing a poor seamstress's costume; Sutherland was
given the tenancy of No. 10 for the first half of the programme and
Schwarzkopf for the rest; whilst Lisa della Casa was coaxed into
changing in the first mezzo-soprano's room as she would be taking
a mezzo role.

Such sweet reasonableness was not always in evidence at that
famous opera house. There was one diva who insisted on all the
furniture in No. 10 dressing-room
being replaced by new pieces before
she would move in, and all because
it would upset her to come into
physical contact with anything
that had been used by a rival.

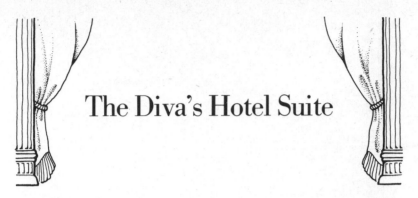

The Diva's Hotel Suite

Trouble, too, could arise as to which diva would occupy the finest suite in a hotel. On one occasion when Colonel Mapleson's company visited Dublin, Mlle Sala, the French soprano, and Mlle Anna De Belocca, the Russian contralto, reached at the same moment such a suite in the hotel where accommodation had been reserved, and each claimed it for herself. This led to a heated dispute and, as neither would yield to the other, they appealed to Mapleson, who went to the manager to enquire whether he had another suite available just as comfortable. He replied that there was one on the second floor, but that both ladies had refused to go any higher than the first.

The impresario thought of a possible way out of the impasse and the manager agreed to co-operate. 'What is the meaning of this?' Mapleson demanded when they were with the rivals. 'This suite will do for one of these ladies, but the other must be provided with one of equal social status. Isn't there one on the next floor usually occupied by the Countess Spencer, the wife of the Lord Lieutenant of Ireland?'

'Yes,' agreed the hotelier, supporting the Colonel's ruse. 'But it is reserved for her exclusive occupation and it would be more than my business is worth to permit anyone else to sleep there.'

Mlle De Belocca became very pensive when she heard this.

'At least we could see it?' asked the impresario.

'You could, but that is all.'

The two men mounted the stairs. The Russian stole after them, and no sooner had the manager unlocked the suite than she slipped past them, slammed and bolted the door behind her shouting, 'Lady Spencer will have to sleep elsewhere should she arrive!'

49

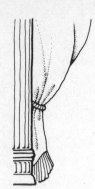
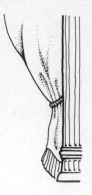

Battles over Billing

Contention can also be caused by billing. 'Artists always see the poster for their rivals but never their own,' states Sir Rudolf Bing, writing from long experience in *5000 Nights at the Opera*. One might add that if rivals who are as egocentric as spinning tops appear in the same opera there is likely to be argument over the position and size of names on the posters and whether, for example, the words 'with' or 'and' should connect them. It was stipulated in Adelina Patti's contract with Colonel Mapleson when she toured the United States that her name in all printed announcements must be at least one-third larger than that of anyone else. In 1885 at the Chicago Festival, her second husband, Ernesto Nicolini, suspected that the wall-posters did not comply with this requirement, so he fetched a ladder, climbed it, watched by a curious crowd, and, using a foot-rule, measured his wife's name and that of the Californian soprano, Emma Nevada. His concern was justified – Adelina's was only a quarter larger, and as a result Mapleson was compelled to have new posters printed.

Male singers, too, have made similar trouble over billing. Mario del Monaco always travelled with a folding rule on his person so that he could measure the size of the names printed on the posters, and if any were in larger type than his own nothing would make him sing till corrections in his favour had been pasted over what had so offended him.

Giuseppe di Stefano, after changing into costume for a performance in Philadelphia's opera house, became enraged when, looking through the programme, he came across an announcement of a coming attraction in which Franco Corelli was described as 'The Greatest Tenor in the World'. Stefano at once shouted: 'I no sing with this insult.' Then, changing back into his own clothes, he announced that he had lost his voice and stalked out to his car pursued by the frantic manager, who implored him with appropriate flattery not to abandon his adoring fans who had already filled every seat in the auditorium and were fighting for standing room. Softened by such unction, Giuseppe hinted that his voice might return if the objectionable pages were torn out of all the programmes and burnt. The management yielded with alacrity.

At the commencement of his career, Stefano had proved far more modest. He was engaged to appear during the season at the Teatro Colòn in Buenos Aires. The star of the company was Gigli, then at the height of his fame, and on one of the posters by mistake his name was printed in much smaller capitals than Stefano's, who was so embarrassed that he went immediately to Gigli to assure him he was in no way responsible for this affront. 'Don't worry, my young friend,' consoled the other, 'as soon as the public hear us both, they will realize which billing is correct.'

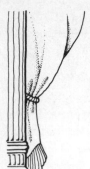
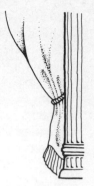

'Spucken Verboten!'

Prima donnas have seldom loved one another, even as far back as the days when Francesca Cuzzoni and Faustina Bordoni Hasse scratched each other's faces in the presence of royalty during a performance at the King's Theatre, London, in 1727. Sometimes the divas have kept their dislike to themselves, behaving as though rivals never existed and carefully avoiding all mention of them in memoirs; and in Victorian times there were those who, despite mutual ill-feeling, were anxious that no one should have cause to accuse them of not being ladies who observed all the rules of polite society.

During Mapleson's American tour of 1883 Adelina Patti and her second husband, Ernesto Nicolini, were staying in the same Detroit hotel as Emma Albani and her husband, Ernest Gye. Soon after their arrival the former couple went out for a drive and Albani caught sight of their carriage passing beneath her window, and exclaimed: 'Ernest, they have gone out. We had better leave cards on them at once.'

On regaining her suite, Patti found these awaiting her, and knowing that Albani had to go to the theatre for a rehearsal, she watched at the window and about an hour later told Nicolini: 'They've gone. Now is the time for returning their call.'

Such discretion is advisable when animosity is intense. Lilian Nordica had an unhappy experience in 1894 at Bayreuth, where she sang Elsa in *Lohengrin*. She attended a reception given by Cosima Wagner at the Villa Wahnfried, and approaching Lilli Lehmann asked if she might call on her. The other replied icily: 'I am not taking any pupils this season.'

Not so rude, but hardly a compliment, were Marguerite

d'Alvarez's greetings to Elena Gerhardt, the great *lieder*-singer, on attending the twenty-fifth anniversary of the latter's début: 'Oh, what a joy it is to meet you. I adore your recitals. But how different an art yours is from mine! Yours is all mid-day sunshine, nature and glorious beer, but mine is midnight candlelight and champagne.'

Divas can be even more disparaging, not face to face, but hoping that their remarks will be reported back to the insulted one or reach a wider public through some popular gossip-writer's column. Emma Eames's assessment of Gatti-Casazza's wife – 'Oh, Alda's fine for the chorus' – was soon common knowledge in operatic circles. Marguerite d'Alvarez's criticism of a rival's Carmen was more colourfully expressed: 'I admit that she sings well but she moves as though her shoes were filled with lead and her castanets have the tone of tired kippers.' Galli-Curci said of Melba: 'When she has finished singing "Lo, hear the gentle lark", you would think you've been listening to a turkey.' And if one wants posterity to be certain of knowing what one thought of another singer it must be mentioned in one's autobiography. Claire Louise Kellogg, remembering in hers Calvé's début in *Faust* at the Théâtre de la Monnaie, Brussels, in 1882, wrote: 'Her Marguerite was a mixture of red pepper and vanilla blanc-mange.'

More subtle is the apparently unintentional insult, such as when Dame Nellie Melba suddenly burst into full song in her suite at the Savoy just when Tetrazzini happened to walk past along the corridor. The latter pretended to shudder and inquired of an employee: 'Have you many cats in your hotel?'

Also at the Savoy, Mary Garden, wearing a perfume especially prepared for her exclusive use, was ushered into the restaurant. Emma Calvé, already seated there, sniffed the air and in a loud voice demanded a table as far away as possible from the other. Then there was the diva who remarked after a rival had just left a party: 'What a woman! Nothing but I – I – I! Talk of a swollen head!' Suddenly a car back-fired out in the street. 'There – it has exploded!'

Emma Eames, who was six years younger than Melba, made her farewell in 1912, whilst the latter carried on singing for another fourteen years. When an acquaintance commented on this, Mme Eames, a famous beauty in her youth, retorted: 'I would rather be a brilliant memory than a – curiosity.'

But insults, direct or indirect, do not really get a prima donna very far. It would be more likely to damage her rivals' careers and further her own if she succeeded in excluding them from the stage of a great opera house, as Melba did at Covent Garden, or in seeing that no one else was allowed to sing what she regarded as *her* roles there.

Christine Nilsson attempted to do this. When in 1873 the London season ended, Mapleson found her reluctant to sign a contract to return the following year. This was due to her jealousy of Thérèse Tietjens's popularity with British audiences. Eventually, however, Christine's agent, Jarrett, persuaded her to sign, but the document was not produced for signature till the Swede was in the boat-train and about to leave Victoria on her way to Paris.

The impresario wanted to read it through first, but Mlle Nilsson cried: 'There isn't time. Either sign or leave it alone. I can make no alterations.'

Confronted with such an ultimatum, Mapleson signed. After her departure he went carefully through his copy of the agreement and discovered that the wily soprano had inserted a clause to the effect that she only would have the right to play Norma, Lucrezia, Fidelio, Donna Anna, Semiramide and Valentine (in *Les Huguenots*). Searching for some way out of his predicament, he noticed that three important words, 'during the season', had been omitted; so, as Nilsson's engagement for 1874 did not begin before 29 May, he was left with a clear eleven weeks during which another singer, without breaking the contract, could sing the roles Christine Nilsson had reserved for herself.

Very concerned about Thérèse Tietjens's reactions, Mapleson confided the position to her. She took it well, saying she had no objections to the Swedish soprano singing the parts in question and that if the public were to prefer her rendering, she could keep the right to sing them in London for the future. But during the first eleven weeks, when no restrictions were in force, Thérèse said she would perform every part so that audiences might judge between them.

The season opened in the manner suggested and Tietjens won 'rave' reviews from the critics. Then Nilsson arrived and sang first in Gounod's *Faust*, then in Balfe's *Talismano*, after which Mapleson informed her that he wished her to appear as Lucrezia.

54

Next morning Christine's agent called and told the impresario she did not feel ready to play the part in London, so Mapleson suggested Semiramide or Fidelio as alternatives. Jarrett then dropped all pretence and declared that if Nilsson were forced to sing any of the roles Tietjens had sung during the first eleven weeks, Mapleson would 'mortally offend' his client. So for the rest of the season Christine limited her repertoire to *Faust* and *Talismano*. But despite this, both critics and public compared her unfavourably with Tietjens.

In the 1920s the Viennese packed the Staatsoper to witness the operatic Olympics in progress on its stage between Maria Jeritza and Lotte Lehmann as each appeared in turn as Elisabeth, Elsa, Sieglinde, Tosca and Turandot, as well as together in *Ariadne auf Naxos, Der Rosenkavalier, Die Frau ohne Schatten, Carmen* and *Die Walküre*. Their admirers kept the auditorium ringing with frenzied cheering and counter-cheering.

In *Die Walküre* Jeritza as Brünnhilde and Lehmann as Sieglinde were joined by another temperamental prima donna, Maria Olczewska, who sang Fricka. This proved unfortunate. There was constant bickering, ending in an unseemly backstage brawl in which the male principals also took part.

An uneasy truce was brought into force, until one evening Mme Olczewska, annoyed by Jeritza's talking in the wings, spat at her in full view of the audience.

A report from the Viennese correspondent of the *Musical Times* for 1 July 1925 ran:

The latest news is that something like harmony has been restored, Mme Olczewska having expressed her 'profound regret for disgracing the dignity of the house, and insulting the public by trying to spit at Madame Jeritza in the wings, missing, and hitting Madame Kittel instead'. We are glad the apology was so ample as to include regret for the deplorable marksmanship.

The incident led to a very successful bit of business on the part of a singer in *The Bartered Bride* at Vienna, a few days later. On receiving the contract confirming the sale of the bride he spat furiously at it with truer aim than that of Madame Olczewska, we trust. The house roared and continued to show its appreciation of the hit (we assume it was a hit) during the remainder of the scene. The director, Herr Schalk, then went behind the curtain, and issued an order that *spucken*, or even imitation thereof, was for ever *verboten* on that stage.

There was trouble in another production of *Die Walküre* when Olive Fremstad and Johanna Gadski, redoubtable rivals for Wagnerian laurels in their day, appeared as Sieglinde and Brünnhilde. Olive wounded her arm on Johanna's metal breastplate but did not allow the injury to affect her acting, and made no attempt to staunch the flow of blood as the two women stood acknowledging the applause at the fall of the curtain. Then as the plaudits died away, she wiped the blood off on Johanna's face.

There has been jealousy, too, between sopranos and tenors. In January 1886 at the Chicago Opera House when Luigi Ravelli, playing Don José, was about to embark on a high note usually received with tremendous applause, Minnie Hauk as Carmen suddenly dashed forward and hugged and kissed him, completely spoiling the effect of his singing. Infuriated, he made as if he were about to hurl her into the orchestra pit and she, to avoid this, clutched his red waistcoat. 'Let go – let go!' he shouted in French, but she would not release her grip till she had ripped off all his buttons, when she retreated to the other side of the stage.

Ravelli then rushed down to the footlights and roared: 'Look – look – she has ruined my waistcoat!' The audience, unaware that his emotion was real, assumed he was acting with magnificent realism and gave him a tumultuous ovation.

But, once the curtain fell, a quarrel in the grand manner broke out between the pair, ending with Ravelli threatening to kill her. As a result, next morning the impresario, Mapleson, received a letter from Minnie Hauk's husband, Baron von Hesse-Wartegg, stating that the tenor's 'vile language, insults and threats' in the presence of the entire company had incapacitated her from singing as she was 'in constant fear of being stabbed'. Minnie would be unable to appear again in public before her health was restored.

The Baron ended: 'Mr. Ravelli can congratulate himself on my absence from the stage, when further scenes would have occurred.' Three days after this, Mapleson received a letter from Minnie Hauk's attorney, threatening to apply to the magistrates for a warrant against Ravelli unless a bond was taken out to guarantee

his future good behaviour, and this the impresario was forced to
do.

In 1881 Mapleson had trouble with the same artist over a new
opera, *Il rinnegato* by Baron Bodoz Orczy, presented at Her
Majesty's Theatre. In the second act there was a duel between the
baritone and the tenor, played by Luigi Ravelli who strongly
objected to the scene where he is killed by the former. 'A tenor,' he
argued, 'accustomed to portraying heroes should not be seen to die
on the stage beneath the sword of a baritone whose usual role is
that of a villain.'

At long last Ravelli was persuaded to see reason, after much
weeping, screaming and threats to kill with his dagger not only the
baritone but everyone in sight. But he yielded only on condition
that six attendants entered and carried his body away with
appropriate solemnity.

The libretto, however, required him to lie still first for a while so
that the soprano could pour out her grief in song over his corpse,
and this he absolutely refused to allow, complaining that he would
have to remain in an inglorious position for ten minutes at least. So
the aria was omitted during the final rehearsals.

At the première, nevertheless, the prima donna remained on the
stage and sang her lament in full over him. Those waiting in the
wings feared that this might madden him, with alarming
consequences. But when at last the attendants were able to remove
him, to everyone's astonishment he remained perfectly calm.
Possibly listening to the long catalogue of noble qualities belonging
to the character he was impersonating had appeased him.

Birgit Nilsson is usually on the best of terms with other singers,
but attempts to steal the show from her have resulted in her hitting
back, and as a result she has been called the diva with *la voce di
vendetta*. Once, at La Scala in the second act of *Turandot*, Franco
Corelli as Calaf held a high C for the *bravura* effect in *'In questa
reggia'*, and did so longer than Birgit who was singing the title role.
At the next performance she retaliated by holding the note so long
that he became out of breath.

Some time later they both appeared in these roles at the
Metropolitan and then toured together. One night in the opera
house at Boston, Mme Nilsson eclipsed Corelli with her powerful
singing in the same duet. This so annoyed him that, having nothing

further to sing for the rest of the act, he walked off the stage and went to his dressing-room saying that he would not appear again that evening.

On learning this, Rudolf Bing went to reason with him. An expert at dealing with difficult artists, the manager told Corelli that his reputation with American audiences would be considerably diminished if they learnt he had let a woman get the better of him. 'Take my advice,' Bing is reported to have said, 'go back in the third act, and when you are supposed to kiss her, *bite* her instead.'

Corelli did as suggested. Meanwhile, Bing had hastily returned to New York. Next day Birgit Nilsson rang him there saying: 'I cannot go on to Cleveland. I have rabies!'

When on tour in the United States, Tito Gobbi took the part of Germont in a radio production of *La traviata*. In his autobiography he reveals that no sooner had he begun singing *'Pura siccome un angelo'* than his Violetta gracefully crossed the stage and, as if by accident, covered the floor microphone with her crinoline, thus muffling and diminishing the sound of his voice. The moment it was her turn to sing she, of course, moved her crinoline off the microphone.

Gobbi adds that during the same broadcast the tenor playing Alfredo threw his arms round him in such a tight bear hug at the close of the aria *'Di provenza'* and shook him so violently that he was almost stifled into silence. However, continues the great baritone, if he could hardly manhandle Violetta, it would be in character to treat his operatic son with firmness. So seizing the latter's wrist with a vice-like grip, he pushed him down on to his knees whilst registering intense parental emotion, and kept him in that position.

Tempers can boil concerning the order of appearance at concerts. When Frances Alda, Albert Spalding and Ignaz Paderewski took part in a morning musicale held in the ballroom of the Biltmore Hotel, the great pianist insisted that the programme should end with his recital. This infuriated the soprano who told the violinist that they must combine to make Paderewski regret his selfishness. She intended to sing encores at every opportunity and Spalding must do the same. The audience consisted mainly of elderly society women and by the time Alda and Albert had finished it was almost one o'clock, and the ladies were feeling hungry and starting to fidget. Then Paderewski's piano had to be placed in the right position and the lighting changed, and he also took his time so as to make an impressive entrance. Those with whom food came first availed themselves of this chance to slip away to the dining-room, so that when the pianist came on to the stage and noticed how few remained in their seats, he told the escaping laggards in the gangway: 'If no one here wants to hear me play, I might as well have my lunch, too.' At which reproof, those on their feet shamefacedly sat down again.

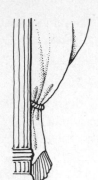
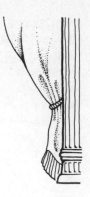

Nightingales in Peacocks' Feathers

Frances Alda always paid much attention to what she wore at concerts so as to create the right mood and render her audience more receptive. Other women singers have done the same. But this should not be carried to extremes. The American prima donna, Emma Nevada, born in Alpha near Nevada City, was the daughter of a physician named Wixon, who had his practice in the city from which she took her stage name. According to the *Musical Times* for January 1886, she changed her dress after every song during the concerts she gave in the States:

On one occasion we are informed that she first appeared in a costume of pale blue silk tastefully embroidered with daisies; afterwards she came forward in a red velvet bodice and overskirt which told with effect against the underskirt of white satin, bearing like the bodice large rose-coloured flowers embroidered in high relief. Then came the wedding dress (of which we have heard so much) that she wore at her marriage in the French capital, a costume almost defying description, but sufficiently distracting in its effect upon the audience to make it doubtful whether the applause which was showered upon her was elicited by her singing or her dress.

Probably the most distracting raiment ever seen on the operatic stage was that of Patti when she sang for the last time at Covent Garden before a rapturous audience that included the Prince and Princess of Wales. In the Ball Scene of the third act of *La traviata* she appeared in a white dress, upon the corsage of which were mounted some four thousand diamonds valued then a $1m and removed for the occasion from the settings of the jewellery acquired during her career. With this she wore several ropes of pearls, bracelets and a tiara. It is not surprising that she needed a detachment of detectives to guard her from when she left the hotel till she returned.

Such a display might be excusable when playing a courtesan such as Violetta, but hardly so in the case of Geraldine Farrar, who, as Marguerite, the peasant heroine in *Faust*, wore showy diamond buckles on her shoes when singing at the Metropolitan – possibly to impress the *nouveaux riches* seated in its 'Diamond Horseshoe'. The American critic Vincent Sheean wrote that she was capable of an exhibitionism which had nothing to do with her role. 'She almost seemed to be winking at the audience as a circus clown does. She liked silks, satins and trains; even the village maiden in *Faust* had acquired a train by the time I saw her, and the dresses for *Madama Butterfly* must have cost a fortune.'

The Canadian contralto Jeanne Gordon longed to sing Carmen at the Met and at last, on 4 April 1925, her wish was granted. Determined to outshine any earlier interpreter of the role, she wore in the last act a magnificent infanta costume which had its skirt stretched over a cage of graduated wire hoops. When Don José, played by Armand Tokatyan, stabbed her, she sank on to the stage with her feet towards the audience, but unfortunately the hoops rose revealing her underwear. The tenor, knife in hand, stared appalled at the sight which was already raising gasps and titters in the stalls. Then with great presence of mind, bemoaning her death, he sat upon the gaping hoops and crushed them, thus proving that despite his crime he was a perfect gentleman.

A prima donna who never made any attempt to show off and who even at the height of her career was willing to appear in supporting roles was the Spanish soprano, Lucrezia Bori, whose real name was Borgia and who was believed to be descended from the notorious Lucrezia. Miss Bori first sang at the Metropolitan in 1912 and scored an immediate success in the title role of Puccini's *Manon Lescaut*.

At the height of her career, this fine singer was afflicted with a throat complaint which no one could cure, and which forced her to retire. Back in Spain, she was one day thrown off her mule when riding in the mountains. She struck her head on the rocks and became unconscious, but on recovering she found that the shock had restored her voice, thus enabling her to return to the operatic stage.

Although it was not her practice to join issue with the critics, on one occasion she did. This was in 1924 when those of the principal American papers all received the following letter:

Dear Sir,

Pardon me for my seeming but innocent effrontery. We Spanish women are not in the habit of writing to newspapers . . . . However, when my kind musical critics take me to task regarding my costumes, I reserve the right to cross swords with them. Some of these critics took serious exception to my costumes as Giulietta, the Venetian courtesan, in the second act of *The Tales of Hoffmann*. I don't think I am mistaken in assuming that they belong to the more serious or sterner sex. Such being the case, as a woman I may be permitted to question their authority as arbiters of the feminine toilette.

Consequently, to show that I bear no malice, I am prepared to give a nice little tea party in honour of the musical critic (male, or course) who will submit to me the best original sketch of a smart eighteenth-century Venetian courtesan's evening frock suitable to the scene in question.

Of course, he must be honor bound to create this design without the aid, direct or indirect, sympathetic or unsympathetic – may I say without the knowledge of his wife or sweetheart.

Naturally the musical critics of fashion journals are not eligible in the contest.

Ernest Newman, who was then a contributor to the *New York Post*, commented in its columns, after receiving a copy of this, that if critics were so abandoned as to take serious exception to Mme Bori's costume, he was not one of them. He had not even noticed it, which was a tribute to her singing, for it was his experience that a music critic's preoccupation with what a singer wore 'varies conversely with his interest in her vocal art'. He remembered a French Tosca who, in the second act, was attired in a frock so tight and so diaphanous that when he came to write his notice he found to his astonishment that he had not the faintest recollection of how she had sung, or, indeed, if she had sung at all.

Newman went on to admit his total inability to design a dress for a Venetian courtesan. He did not know whether critics ought to regard Mme Bori's assumption of acquaintance on their part with such subjects as a reflection on their morals or a tribute to their taste. But there had been occasions when even he had ventured to have an opinion.

I have never been able to understand how rough and starving peasant women always manage to look as if they had stepped straight out of a beauty parlour – judging from the evidence of the forest scene in *Boris Godounov* – or how Manon in Puccini's opera managed to tramp the rough prairie for all those weary miles in satin shoes without either hurting her feet or damaging the shoes; or how Wotan and Fricka, in the second scene of the Rhinegold, sometimes manage to have gold ornaments about them before the existence of gold is known to the gods . . . .

As for oratorio, could anything be more absurd, he asked, than *Elijah* in evening dress or the *Daughter of Zion* in a transformation? 'Would not oratorio singers put more realism into their work if they were properly garbed? For my part, if I had the power I would insist on all oratorio being sung in the costume of the period – with a possible exception in the case of the Creation.'

Blanche Marchesi would not have agreed with Newman. Evening dress in her opinion was essential when singing in oratorio. In *A Singer's Pilgrimage* she wrote about having often seen women taking part clad in short skirts covered with spangles, with a sleeveless bodice held over the shoulders by strings of beads, and with their hair bobbed. This she regarded as altogether unsuitable.

When the famous Mme Mathilde's daughter started giving recitals, she wondered what to wear. So she visited Jean Worth, the celebrated *couturier*, who, after listening to her mixed programme of dramatic and humorous songs, made a heavy black crêpe de Chine dress, perfectly simple and beautiful in line, to be worn at her afternoon concerts and the same in white for the evening. Despite the prevailing fashion, she wore no gloves because she felt that they impeded the movements of her hands when trying to express feeling.

In London and Paris these gowns created a tremendous impression, but at a Gewandhaus concert in Leipzig, where she appeared for a change in the black dress in the evening, it was not appreciated. Two men representing the committee of management visited her during the interval and said that the ladies in the hall all wondered if she were in mourning.

Blanche replied that she certainly wasn't and that in both the

British and French capitals her attire had been admired by audiences and praised in the press.

The men stared incredulously at her, then the elder of the two asked: 'May I touch the material? Is it silk? It looks like wool from a distance.'

'It's double *crêpe de Chine cuir* and cost sixteen hundred francs,' Blanche retorted.

'You don't really mean that?' exclaimed the younger man. 'It looked quite a cheap dress, and the ladies always expect at this concert to see some new fashion.'

'Well, when I came to sing at the Gewandhaus I really did not dream in entering this holy of holies of music that my dress would be discussed at all and especially that it would be criticized,' Blanche claims she retorted angrily. 'If you had come to the green-room to discuss my songs I would have understood, but my dress! This surpasses everything I could have imagined.'

And next day, records the singer sadly, the critic of the principal paper in Leipzig had not a good word to say about her performance.

Some singers consider that the greatest aid to successful characterization is a convincing wig, and this was especially true with Mary Garden, who took immense pains over the impressive display of dark-red hair that transformed her into Tosca for her New York début in that role on 2 December 1912. This contrasted admirably with the emerald-green dress and the deep-blue head scarf she wore in the church scene, and in the second act with her clinging empire gown of silver and white – so telling when seen against Scarpia's black satin.

The wig of which Mary Garden was most proud was the strikingly long blond one she donned as Mélisande, the strands of which came from a careful poll of girls in Brittany. It has been said that on lecture tours Mary would sometimes exhibit this hirsute glory, saying: 'You must love it to be Mélisande.'

Wigs are of importance even to members of the chorus, for on occasion they can steal the attention of the audience away from the star. In *A Voice, a Life*, Joan Hammond tells how at the commencement of her career in Australia, during the first act of *Madama Butterfly* when she was playing one of the heroine's companions, quite suddenly the top of her head felt chilly and, looking up, she saw her Japanese wig dangling from a branch of a blossoming cherry tree, which had pierced the bun on top. Overcome with embarrassment, she bowed hurriedly to the others, fluttered her fan frantically, and tottered into the wings. The stage manager glared and she feared he would fire her, but he only grumbled: 'Gor blimey, Hammond, can't you keep your ruddy roof on?'

Such mishaps can spoil a performance, and so, too, can lack of attention to details in costuming. After another production of the same opera, John McCormack told the Yorkshire tenor who had played Lieutenant Pinkerton: 'You sang very well, but you must have been a rotten naval officer.'

'Why?' demanded the other.

'You began with a little bit of gold braid on your sleeve,' explained the Irishman. 'Then years later, when you return to Japan and your little Butterfly, you're still wearing the same bit of braid. Don't you ever get promoted? When I sang Pinkerton, I took good care to promote myself to Commander in the third act.'

Even Caruso could be similarly careless. When he appeared as Dick Johnson in the Metropolitan première of the *The Girl of the Golden West* in 1910, it was noticed that he had put his spurs on the wrong way up.

Writing in *Musical America* in 1968 about 'grand opera grotesqueries', Robert Sabin recalled how in a Metropolitan production of *Norma*, when Rosa Ponselle in the title role came on to the stage accompanied by vestal virgins in sweeping and somewhat soiled white robes, he was startled to see that several of them were very noticeably in the family way. Clearly the bad example set by the High Priestess in breaking her vows of chastity had affected the morals of her sisterhood.

This marred the performance for Sabin and despite Ponselle's superb singing he became aware of other defects; the long-johns visible through chinks in Pollione's armour; the shoddy state of the Roman soldiers' weapons; the vastness of Norma's bedchamber, more like a main railway station; and the anachronistic variety of hairstyles among the Druids.

Convincing costumes can contribute greatly in bringing opera to life. David Franklin relates how at Glyndebourne for the dress rehearsal of *Don Giovanni* he put on for the first time the costume he had to wear as the statue of the Commendatore in Act II. This proved extremely uncomfortable, being made of heavy canvas, stiffened with size, so that it looked as if the folds were carved in marble, and the smell emanating from it made the others keep as far away from him as possible. Carl Ebert, the producer, and Hamish Wilson, the designer, were disappointed with the stone effect, and after consulting together in an undertone, they led Franklin to a wall and told him to stand against it. When the singer asked why, Wilson replied: 'You'll find out. And close your eyes.'

Franklin obeyed. Then the designer dipped a whitewash brush into a pail, and flicked it at him from a range of about 6 feet.

'What the hell was that for?' spluttered the victim furiously, wiping a dollop of whitewash from one eye.

'You're a statue, aren't you?' the other retorted.

'All right, I'm a statue,' Franklin agreed, 'so what?'

'Pigeons,' explained the satisfied designer.

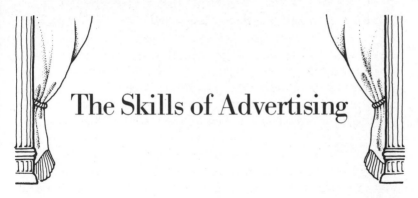

The Skills of Advertising

David Franklin's anecdote about his costume as the Commendatore is just the kind of story which a lively PRO might pass on to a gossip-columnist so as to gain publicity for a production. This is by no means new to this century. Patti at the commencement of her career was managed by her brother-in-law impresario, Maurice Strakosch. It has been said that she found the right man at the right moment and that he found the right star at the right time of his life. He proved a master of publicity. No one could approach him in the invention of astonishing tales with which to add savour to the breakfasts of the bourgeoisie as they scanned their newspapers.

One learned that at the end of a farewell concert somewhere in South America, Adelina had been presented with twelve black slaves in chains and that, flooding the stage with tears, she broke loose their fetters with her own hands crying that she was giving them their freedom. Whereupon the rejoicing dozen knelt and kissed her tiny feet, and the entire audience rose and cheered and clamoured for her to sing 'Home Sweet Home'.

Another morning the front page would reveal that the diva owed her incomparable voice to the fact that each night as a bed-time snack she ate a sandwich enriched with the tongues of twelve nightingales.

True, however, was the report that an admirer had given her an exquisitely made little mechanical bird and that she could not sleep without having it beside her; on waking, she would wind it up, taking its high notes, trills and runs for a model.

The king of nineteenth-century showmen, Barnum, had no equal in the art of publicity. Before Jenny Lind arrived in the United States on her concert tour, he had already aroused in the public feverish excitement and a desire to hear her sing whatever the cost. He saw to it that the New York papers contained highly exaggerated descriptions of her departure from Liverpool, with guns saluting from the shores whilst tearful thousands waved goodbye, led by Queen Victoria who had come incognito to bid farewell to her favourite friend, whose most cherished possession was the nightingale fashioned entirely out of gems the royal lady had once given her to wear in her hair – this at least was true. And to attract the deeply religious, inclined to regard theatres and opera houses as the devil's playground, he stressed that Jenny would sing only at concerts. His press handout declared that her character was 'charity, simplicity and goodness personified'. It continued: 'Since her début in England she has given to the poor from her own private purse more than the whole amount which I have engaged to pay her, and the proceeds of concerts for charitable purposes in Great Britain where she has sung gratuitously have realized more than ten times that amount.' Later Barnum was to claim that 'little did the public see of the hand that indirectly pulled at their heart-strings preparatory to a relaxation of their purse-strings'.

As a result of this build-up, some 30,000 people were at the dockside to greet the 'Swedish Nightingale' when she arrived in New York to the most enthusiastic reception ever given to a European celebrity, and the receipts from her first six concerts totalled $87,055.89. There followed in other cities sixty more concerts, equally profitable.

Hector Berlioz in his *Evenings with the Orchestra* satirized Barnum's methods in an imaginary conversation with 'Winter, the American, who nobody knows why is second bassoon. Just look at what they were saying':

When she [Lind] landed at New York, the crowd rushed after her so wildly that hundreds of people were crushed and collapsed unconscious on the dockside. The survivors were nevertheless sufficient in number to prevent her carriage from leaving. It was then that, seeing her coachman raising his arm to whip off these foolish admirers, Jenny Lind uttered the sublime words now repeated from Upper Canada right down to Mexico, words that bring tears to the eyes of all who hear them quoted: 'Don't strike, don't strike! They are my friends, they have come to see me.' One hardly knows what to admire in these unforgettable sentiments – the heart-felt impulse that inspired it, or the genius that clothed the thought in so fine and noble a choice of words. Rapturous cheering naturally rewarded her thoughtful gesture. . . .

In the centre of the quay stood a triumphal arch of green branches surmounted with a stuffed eagle, which seemed to be waiting to greet her. At midnight the orchestra of the Philharmonic Society serenaded her and for two hours the famous songstress was compelled to remain at her window braving the chilly night air. Next day Mr. Barnum, the clever bird-catcher, who has succeeded in caging the Swedish nightingale for a few months, took her to his Museum, all the curiosities of which he showed her . . . and finally holding up a mirror before the goddess so that she could catch her reflexion, he said with superb gallantry: 'This, Madesmoiselle, is at present the rarest and most exquisite exhibit we have to show you.'

As she left the Museum, a choir of young and pretty girls, dressed in virginal white, escorted her singing hymns and scattering flowers in her path. . . . Meanwhile dolphins and whales which for more than eight hundred leagues had followed her ship . . . were disporting themselves frantically outside the port, in despair because they could not accompany her ashore. Seals shedding huge tears were bellowing the most mournful lamentations. There followed a spectacle dearer still to her heart – gulls and other ocean birds circled fearlessly about the adorable creature, perching on her pure shoulders . . . bearing in their bills enormous pearls which they presented to her most courteously, cooing gently the while. The guns thundered, the bells pealed *Hosanna!* to her, and at intervals awesome claps of thunder reverberated through a radiant *cloudless* sky.

All this, Berlioz comments, 'which is as unquestionably true as the marvellous things done long ago by Amphion and Orpheus, is doubted only by us old Europeans, effete as we are, tired of pleasure, without passion and without love for art'.

Continuing in this vein, the composer wrote that Barnum considered 'this spontaneous demonstration of affectionate admiration by the creatures of nature was still inadequate a tribute to be paid the singing enchantress, so he went so far as to recourse to a little innocent charlatanry.' Berlioz continued:

Hearing of the penury of several New York families and wishing to associate Jenny Lind's arrival with some memorable act of financial generosity he said to the heads of these families in distress: 'When one has lost everything, and there is no longer any hope, life becomes an unbearable burden, and you know what remains for you to do. Well, I am offering you an opportunity of doing so in a way profitable to your miserable children and your wretched wives, who will ever more be grateful to you. *She* has arrived!!!'

'She, who?'

'Yes, *she*, her own self. I therefore guarantee your heirs two thousand dollars to be paid to them in full the day the deed which you are contemplating takes place – so long as you perform it in the way I shall now describe to you. Now listen: some of you will have only to climb to the top floor of the houses near the concert hall and fling yourselves on to the pavement below when she passes, shouting: 'Long live Lind!' Others are to hurl themselves with stoically calm decorum under her horses' hoofs or under the wheels of her carriage. The rest will be admitted without having to pay a cent to the hall where she is singing. . . . At the end of her second cavatina they will loudly proclaim that after listening to her the humdrum routine of their lives is no longer bearable and they will proceed to stab themselves through the heart with the daggers I have here. No pistols, I must insist, for they are weapons unworthy of her, and moreover she might find the noise offensive to her sensitive ears.'

'The bargain was struck and its terms would certainly have been faithfully carried out by both parties to the agreement had not the American police, a meddlesome and unenlightened force if ever there was one, intervened to frustrate the scheme. . . . And so it was that the 'death claque' was not put into practice and a number of poor people were denied a new way of earning their living by dying.

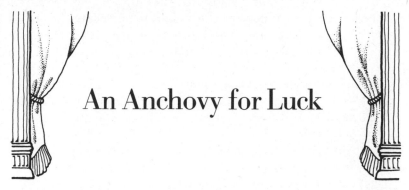

An Anchovy for Luck

All the efforts of a PRO to attract public attention cannot, of course, ensure full houses. Artists themselves often place far more faith in amulets and auguries. There is a tradition among opera singers that to wish anyone good luck before a first night will have the opposite effect. Many prefer to say instead *'Merde'* or *'In bacco del lupo'* ('Into the wolf's mouth') or 'Break your leg'. This is based on the belief that Fate is a double-dealer and that if you regard ill-fortune as probable you can outwit her.

Although Caruso smoked up to sixty cigarettes a day, he was convinced his health would not suffer as long as he kept a dried anchovy suspended over his chest by a chain from his neck. His life was ruled by respect for superstitions. Never on a Friday would he travel or wear a new suit – and before putting one on for the first time he would slip a coin into the right-hand pocket.

Rivalling the great tenor in this way was his favourite prima donna, Tetrazzini, who interpreted finding a needle on the floor, or the crossing of her path by a priest or a nun or a hunchbacked woman, as warning signals of imminent disaster. Nothing would ever make her sleep in a hotel room or a cabin bearing the number eight. On the other hand, she believed good luck was around the corner if she met a hunchbacked man or a soldier with a friar carrying an umbrella, or a waggon full of hay drawn by a white horse. Before the curtain rose on a first night, she would drop a silver dagger thrice on to the stage, and if it stuck in the boards every time, she regarded this as the happiest of auguries – rarely did she miss, for the point was sharp and her aim accurate.

Maria Callas, fondling a miniature of the Madonna, the gift of her husband, Meneghini, would cross herself thrice with outstretched

71

fingers in Catholic fashion before making her first entry. But when she left him for Onassis, who belonged to the Greek Orthodox Church, she crossed herself with bunched up fingers instead – in the manner of that Church.

Selma Kurz was convinced that chimney-sweeps brought one good luck, so when she was singing in Vienna the opera house manager would hire one to await her arrival and stroll past the stage door as if by chance. After this had occurred a number of times, she grew so delighted that one day she tried to tip him, but the sweep, being a man of high principle, refused saying: 'It isn't necessary, *meine Dame*, I have been paid already.'

Most prima donnas consider themselves to be unique, so it is only natural that each should select an entirely new way for ensuring good luck. Emma Trentini insisted on Oscar Hammerstein presenting her with half a dollar before she appeared on the stage; Christine Nilsson made anyone available in the wings press her thumbs before the audience first saw her; and Pauline Donalda would tear a button from her costume, which had to be sewn on again after the performance so that she could pull it off next evening.

Dressing-rooms can truly be described as shrines to superstition. No other performer entering one must ever dare to whistle or look over the occupant's shoulder into the mirror. Make-up boxes must remain cluttered. A friend of mine was nearly savaged by a soprano when he attempted to tidy hers and suggested throwing away her lucky but very moth-eaten rabbit's foot.

Mascots kept by singers cover a wide variety of animals. Lucine Amara was never without her old teddy bear, and Leonie Rysanek never without the 'Meenie' Mouse bought in Disneyland the day she heard of her engagement to play Lady Macbeth at the Met, whilst Antonietta Stella always had a stuffed monkey named Joko on her dressing-table. Scotti would have his treasured rag doll by him, Giorgio Tozzi his bronze snail 'Emerson', whilst Giovanni Martinelli surrounded himself with photographs of his wife and family, and to bring good luck kissed each in turn before making his first entrance. Once in *Aida* at Newark in the United States, he remembered on reaching the stage that he had forgotten to kiss one child's picture, so ran off to do this, forcing the orchestra to repeat the refrain till he reappeared.

An Anchovy for Luck

It is a common belief that the more disastrous the dress rehearsal, the brighter the prospects for the première, and the tag line must never be uttered until then. The very first entrance can be an unnerving ordeal. If the door sticks – or one trips on the threshold – or one's costume catches in the scenery – or, worst of all, a black cat crosses from wing to wing, then the curtain might as well be rung down straight away. Curiously enough, if a singer later falls down, that is considered extremely lucky.

Superstition can even cast a shadow over the box-office itself, where the sight of any young person at the head of the queue waiting to buy tickets for a première may make the management shudder, for it means a short run, whereas a senior citizen signifies a long one – most welcome, no doubt, would be an octogenarian.

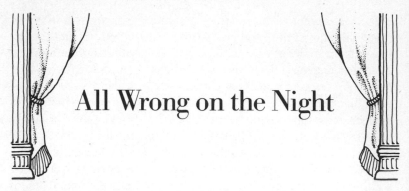

All Wrong on the Night

It is only natural that before a performance singers should above all fear losing their voices and therefore take every precaution against such a disaster happening. Although Jean de Reszke was popular with women, they found close contact with him somewhat trying for he always reeked of the ether and iodoform with which he treated his throat.

Caruso not only equipped himself with atomizers, all sorts of gargling fluids, cold and cough preventives and cures, but obsession with his health extended to medicaments for headaches and migraines, and to avoid catching any skin complaint he took everywhere with him his own linen. Before he occupied a hotel suite, it had to be sprayed first with disinfectant then with the perfume he brought with him for that purpose. He would take a bath and change his clothes after walking in the street or being in close contact with strangers in a public place – and before going to bed he saw that a mattress and piles of pillows were arranged around it on the floor lest he should fall in his sleep and injure himself. Caruso was indeed the King of Operatic Hypochondriacs and one wonders how he would have coped with all the health and other hazards of life in, say, the eighteenth century.

In those times, for example, mishaps were more likely to arise on first nights than they are today, such as on 16 January 1798, when at the Theatre Royal, Drury Lane, there was presented an English version of the successful French opera, *Blue Beard*, with new music composed by Michael Kelly. Although mounted with magnificence, horseplay by the stage carpenter and trouble with the effects almost wrecked the première. At the end, when Blue Beard had been slain by Selim, the corpse of the uxorious one should have disappeared from sight through a trap-door in the stage, and in its place a skeleton should have risen and hovered in the air for a moment or two before sinking again into the realms of darkness. But on this fateful occasion not one inch would the skeleton move; it remained firmly fixed to view long after its appointed period on earth.

Kelly, who as Selim had just been killing Blue Beard, totally forgot himself, rushed up with his drawn sabre and slashed at the poor skeleton's head until it suddenly vanished – and as he did so, forgetting in his annoyance that the audience would catch what he said, he rasped: 'Damn you! Damn you! Why don't you go down?' There were roars of laughter at this ridiculous scene, but the spectators sympathized with the feelings of the infuriated composer-actor, who was very popular. And at the end Miss De Camp (later Mrs Charles Kemble), who was playing the heroine, sang the song, 'I see them galloping! I see them galloping!' with such irresistible verve as to win enormous applause. Her startling scream of excitement and the way she waved her handkerchief as she sighted the rescuers created a sensation. The next day all the faults of machinery were put right and the piece settled down to a profitable run, retaining a place in the repertory for twenty-six years.

Trap-doors have been known to jam on more than one occasion. In Dublin when Mapleson was presenting Gounod's *Faust*, this occurred and Mephistopheles failed to disappear, whereupon a wag in the gallery bawled: 'Three cheers, boys! Hell's full!' A similar shout came from a member of the audience at the Vienna State Opera in 1958 when the stage lift stuck, refusing to remove Cesare Siepi, playing Don Giovanni, to the nether regions.

Trouble with other equipment can also lead to unintended amusement. Eugene Goosens relates how one evening during a performance of *Götterdämmerung* all went well until the dramatic moment in the last act when Brünnhilde orders Siegfried's funeral pyre to be built and, placing the Ring on her finger, rides Grane into the flames. The stage was then darkened for a few seconds so that the backcloth depicting the destruction of Valhalla by fire could be lowered. But when the lights went up, owing to some mechanical fault, nothing could be seen of the cloth except for a tangled corner drooping over an otherwise clear view of the brick wall at the back of the opera house. On this was painted in huge letters: 'NO SMOKING.'

Well known to those familiar with opera lore is the story first told in his reminiscences by Leo Slezak, the Czech tenor, of how after singing his 'Farewell' in *Lohengrin* he walked towards the boat drawn by a swan, but the backstage staff made it move away too soon and he was unable to board it. With admirable presence of mind he strolled towards the audience and inquired: 'Tell me, please, what time is the next swan?'

Sometimes strikes disrupt opera houses. During Sir Joseph Beecham's Grand Season of Russian Opera and Ballet at the Theatre Royal, Drury Lane, in 1914, Fedor Chaliapin triumphed as Boris Godounov and as a result an extra performance was arranged. The Russian chorus, however, was very disgruntled about its poor rate of pay and thought Chaliapin responsible for the management's meanness. All began smoothly with their singing 'God Save the King' followed by the prologue, but when the Coronation Scene was reached they refused to go on to the stage and, with only a few English choristers appearing, what should have proved the spectacular highlight of the evening misfired.

When the curtain fell on this scene Chaliapin, wearing his crown and rich robes, rushed off the stage in a rage, cursing the chorus-leader who had planned the strike and hitting him so hard with his fists that the man collapsed. At this, the whole Russian chorus picked up the staves they had borne in the prologue and charged at Chaliapin, whom they knocked down on to the boards. He would very likely have been battered to death had not the mezzo-soprano Patenka shielded him with her body. The stage-hands then carried him to his dressing-room and locked the door to prevent him resuming the fight. Meanwhile, policemen from Bow Street, summoned by the stage-door keeper, arrived and mounted guard for the rest of the performance, whilst the great bass, before leaving his dressing-room, put a loaded revolver in both pockets.

After the end of the opera there were further heated arguments between Chaliapin and the strikers. Then he suddenly changed his tactics and spoke to them so placatingly, paying such compliments to their singing, that they flung themselves at him, this time to hug and to kiss.

The peace-making was made permanent by the arrival of

Donald Bayliss, Sir Joseph Beecham's general manager, with a
bag of gold sovereigns, and he proceeded to distribute one each to
the Russian choristers. Everybody remained in the theatre
drinking tea until 5 a.m. and indulging in a veritable orgy of
goodwill.

Another occasion when a strike caused a crisis in an opera
house was during the régime of Heinrich Conried at the Met from
1903 to 1908. The chorus formed a union and took industrial
action for the first time, but the operas went on being presented as
before through the principal singers, when not performing their
own roles, assembling in the wings and singing as choristers. As a
result, during a performance of *Tristan und Isolde* there was an
all-star choral ensemble led by Caruso and Nordica, probably the
best in the annals of opera. When after three days the strike was
settled, Conried had gold medals made as souvenirs of the event,
and Caruso wore one on his watch-chain which he would show to
people and joke about the time he spent in the chorus.

The manners of the audience can contribute immeasurably to
the success or failure of a first night. There is the resting prima
donna who, during her rival's great aria, distracts attention from
the stage by losing a diamond bracelet and hunting for it with a
whirling flashlight. Henry Taylor Parker, critic of the *Boston
Transcript*, who signed his reviews 'HTP' and was known as 'Hell
To Pay', became so irritated by the chattering of a couple behind
him one evening that he turned round and told them: 'Those people
on the stage are making so much noise I can't hear a word you're
saying.'

Ivor Newton, who was Grace Moore's accompanist during a
concert tour of Britain, relates in *At the Piano* how, during her
opening group of songs in a packed Leeds cinema on a Sunday
afternoon, the audience became inattentive and disappointed
because she was vocally off-colour. They rustled their programmes
and there was an epidemic of coughing.

'That coughing is driving me crazy,' she complained as they left
the stage. 'I'm going to talk to them about it.' So on returning she
went down to the footlights and with irresistible charm said: 'In
America a few months ago I gave a concert in a hospital for
consumptives. Everyone in that audience was ill and suffering
from that terrible disease but throughout the whole time I was

singing I didn't hear one single cough. Now you all look radiantly healthy – I've never seen an audience look so well – and I've never heard so much coughing in my life.'

Newton writes that her little speech was received with much laughter, shook the audience into attention and herself into concert form. For the rest of the afternoon she sang at her best and there was not a single cough.

What, besides an ill-mannered audience, strikes and mechanical mishaps, can wreck a singer's performance?

When singing the title role in *Lucia di Lammermoor*, Mme Miolhan-Carvalho used to order hot soup from a restaurant near the Paris Opéra which she would sip between the acts. One evening a kitchen-maid was ordered to take it to the prima donna. Not finding the singer in her dressing-room, the girl wandered about backstage till through a gap in the scenery she saw her quarry. Lucia and Ravenswood were on the point of embarking on the impassioned finale to the first act when the maid entered, carrying the tureen which she placed on a mossy bank, and then, lifting the cover, she curtsied and said: 'Begging your pardon, sir, for interrupting you and the lady, but here's the soup.'

Few prima donnas lack self-confidence, but when it comes to competing with animals for the public's attention, they know in advance who will win. Before the opera house was built in Dallas, a huge fairground building was used for performances. Mary Garden in her reminiscences relates how when she attended rehearsals there and the orchestra started playing, hundreds of birds flew out at the first blast of the instruments and 'the musicians had to get popguns and pop the birds out of the windows'. In another city a circus normally performed in the hall where the company was to appear for two nights only, during which time the animals were kept in the cellar. On the first night, suddenly during the love duet between Mimì and Rodolfo in *La Bohème* an enormous red tongue came corkscrewing through a hole in the stage. It belonged to a giraffe curious to discover what was causing the disturbance above. For some seconds the conductor, Campanini, and the two singers were terrified that the creature might break out on to the stage, but to their relief the tongue disappeared from view and the stage manager and his staff hurried below to take the inquisitive intruder elsewhere.

Mary Garden was filmed in the title role of *Thaïs* by Sam Goldwyn. In one scene, to her amazement, the director told her to walk along a path in a garden set between two rows of parrots on their perches and shouted, 'Scratch their heads!'

'You're not serious?' she protested.

'Scratch their heads!' he repeated.

'All of them?' she queried, for there were thirty of them.

'Each and every one of them.'

Mary Garden continues: 'And scratch their heads I did, for one hundred and twenty shots during the silent days. Now they can talk and act and give out their sentiments. But in those days you could do nothing but walk around.'

Years later, however, Grace Moore agreed with alacrity when asked to act with a cow in *The King Steps Out*, and the animal certainly looked in the film as though it was thoroughly enjoying her singing of high Cs.

Then, to promote the musical, she went by train from Hollywood to New York, stopping at important towns on the way to be interviewed about how she had achieved the remarkable feat of milking a cow and at the same time singing a high C. Thus Miss Moore kept her picture on the front pages of the leading newspapers for three days.

Another way to overcome animal competition is to imitate them. Rossini used to copy the sound of a cat every night at about 3 a.m. outside the house of his mistress to let her know when to unfasten the door. This inspired him to compose his *'Duetto buffo di due gatti'*, better known as the 'Comic Duet for Two Cats', which, recorded by Elisabeth Schwarzkopf and Victoria de los Angeles, has proved one of the most popular operatic records ever issued. Ravel, too, wrote a duet for cats in *L'Enfant et les sortilèges*, and Stravinsky wrote *Three Cats' Lullabies*. (Tchaikovsky's *Sleeping Beauty* has a feline *pas de deux*, whilst as a result of his pet jumping on to the keyboard of his harpsichord, Scarlatti wrote the *Cat's Fugue*.)

A variety hall in Exeter became notorious for disturbances caused by animals. On one occasion two elephants were left chained in the basement and no sooner had the orchestra begun playing the overture to *Hänsel und Gretel* than the whole building shook. When the members of the company went down to investigate, the animals were innocently munching hay. However, hardly had the curtain risen on the first scene than the performers found the floor rocking beneath them. This time stage-hands caught the elephants slapping the heating boiler with their trunks, and so as to distract the culprits a man stayed behind throwing hay at them for the rest of the opera.

Insects, too, can be a nuisance. Elisabeth Söderstrom took part in an opera performed one cold night in the People's Park in Kramfors, Sweden, and at the end of the first act she and six other artists moved down-stage for the finale. Their breaths created a misty veil between them and the audience, and to make things worse they noticed in the beam cast by the spotlight a swarm of midges. Ensemble singing forces vocalists to take deep breaths, but they carried on undaunted. Miss Söderstrom says she swallowed seven of the pests.

A mist of a different kind once made playing Pamina in *The Magic Flute* at the Swedish Opera House an ordeal for this soprano. The director, Harold André, was determined to create the eeriest effect possible for the scene in the Temple of Isis, so he had it enveloped in dense mist. When the artists sang the trio in which Pamina bids farewell to Tamino before he undergoes his trials, they coughed more than they sang, so Miss Söderstrom protested to André, who replied: 'Oh, if it troubles you, then I have to tell you it is ammonium chloride we're burning, the stuff the throat specialists use to cure sore throats. It's very good for you.'

So the mists remained.

'*Before you go on, darling, there is just ONE small point – we're doing Madame Butterfly tonight!*'

Webdale

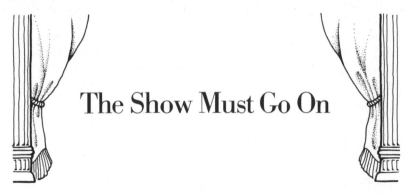

The Show Must Go On

Despite such mists and similar trials singers true to their profession courageously carry on. The 'Florentine Nightingale' ranks high among those deserving praise in this respect. In 1911, following her triumphant seasons at Covent Garden and Oscar Hammerstein's Manhattan Opera House, Luisa Tetrazzini, then aged 40, went on a concert tour of the United States under the management of 'Doc' Leahy, general manager of the old Tivoli Opera House in San Francisco, with André Benoist as accompanist. The latter in his autobiography says that he found working with her a trying experience. She would rehearse only once before the first engagement and then confined this to singing in half-voice the cadenzas with which she embellished her arias. In the middle of the afternoon on the day itself, Leahy phoned Benoist in a state of near-panic. Tetrazzini was suffering from a severe attack of cramp and could hardly move, and every one of the 6,500 seats in the Dreamland Skating Rink had been sold. 'I'm ruined!' he moaned. The soprano had said she would sing despite her illness, but he did not see how she could.

At the time arranged, the anxious pianist went to Tetrazzini's dressing-room and found her hunched up on a chair, head on knees, whilst her feet were pressed against the edge of the seat. Perspiration beaded her face and under the make-up she was a bad colour. Forcing his voice to sound optimistic, he asked how she felt. In broken English she replied: 'Ah no fella good but Ah singa, Ah allaways singa!'

Then Leahy came in and quavered: 'Luisa, it is time.'

With a tremendous effort, she managed to stand and, forcing a smile, made her way slowly to the stage. At the sight of her, the audience went wild with enthusiasm and she responded valiantly with a low curtsy. Benoist approached ready to catch her if she collapsed, but she managed to straighten herself without his help, though he detected beneath the assumed smile the pain she was suffering.

She began with *'Caro nome'* from *Rigoletto* and Benoist writes that never had he witnessed such an astounding display of beauty of tone, admirable technique and true heroism. 'Her roulades and trills came forth perfectly, and she ended with the high E which she attacked pianissimo, started for the exit door and, as she approached it, swelled the E until it sounded like a clarion. She held it as she bowed low and disappeared.'

Tetrazzini had triumphed once again, and the audience saluted her with applause that it seemed would never end. Back in the dressing-room, she sat up on the chair as before and told Benoist: 'Ah no fella good, but Ah singa, Ah allaways singa!' And in this fashion she completed the programme, resting at length between each song.

Seven years previously the 'Florentine Nightingale' had given an earlier example of a different kind of pluck. In the winter of 1904 she had been singing for a pittance in Mexico City with a fourth-rate opera company, when 'Doc' Leahy first heard her and was so impressed that he offered her a contract to star with his company. The Mexican management refused to release her and called in the police to prevent her from leaving the country.

So Luisa resorted to a desperate stratagem to escape. Still fairly slim, she disguised herself convincingly in male clothes, stuck on a false moustache, scraped her hair up on top of her head in a bun, hid it under a sombrero, and succeeded in boarding a steamer without being recognized. She was congratulating herself on her achievement when shouts revealed that the police were searching the ship for a woman.

Fearing that she might be recognized, Luisa rushed to the nearest lavatory and joined the men standing at the urinal, so that all her pursuers saw when they glanced inside was her back. Thus she escaped to San Francisco, where her subsequent sensational success led to a career that took her to the operatic heights.

Tetrazzini could always turn awkward moments to her advantage, such as when her flowing gown caught on a nail on the stage and she bent down gracefully to unhook it while holding a high C, and thus gained an ovation. Robert Hichens in his memoirs tells how once when he went to hear her in the Albert Hall, he sat in the front row and next to him was a lady with a bad cold who as Luisa was about to embark on her first aria gave a resounding sneeze. Quite unperturbed, the diva bowed to the other and said in English: 'Bless you, my de–ar.' Then she calmly went on to sing.

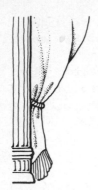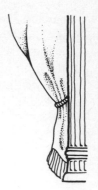

The Programme

Let us now settle down in the opera house awaiting the rise of the curtain. We leaf through the programme, casting a sceptical eye at the advertisements. These have a useful function in so far as they help with the cost of printing the programmes but they can be distracting if not kept in their proper place. Leo Slezak gives an example of this in his autobiography, *Song of Motley*. He was appearing in the title role of Verdi's *Otello* in the opera house at Houston, Texas, and according to him the argument for Act One was set out like this:

[A Port in Cyprus]
The populace are kneeling in prayer for Othello whose ship is in great danger in a violent tempest at sea. The peril is overcome. Othello enters and greets the people with the words:
DO ALL YOUR COOKING WITH 'KRUSTO' THE FAMOUS COOKING-FAT
'Let all rejoice! The Turk is overthrown and cast into the sea.' The people cheer Othello.
'KRUSTO' IS THE ONLY COOKING-FAT YOU CAN USE
Iago, jealous of Cassio, who enjoys the favour of Othello, makes him intoxicated. A drinking song
ANYBODY WHO TRIES COOKING WITHOUT 'KRUSTO' IS CRAZY
is heard and Cassio, already under the influence of wine, attacks Montano, sword in hand. There is a great noise and Othello enters and calls out in a terrible voice:
'KRUSTO' HAS NO RIVALS
'Down with your swords!' Cassio is deposed from his captaincy, as

84

Desdemona, the adored wife of Othello, appears in the gateway of the castle. Othello goes forward to meet her and they both sing a lovely duet
WHOEVER HAS USED 'KRUSTO' WILL NEVER USE ANY OTHER FAT
which is generally considered to be one of the gems of opera music. This concludes Act I.

Exhortations to use 'Krusto' are similarly inserted in the summaries for the remaining three acts and at the end one reads:

Having strangled Desdemona, Othello stabs himself in the breast and while dying, sings the moving words:
ALWAYS INSIST ON 'KRUSTO' THE ONLY GENUINE COOKING-FAT
'Kiss me, kiss me once again' – and expires.

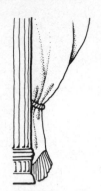
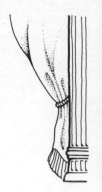

Realism in Opera

We look up from our programmes as the overture commences. The critics have stressed that this is a particularly realistic production – the kind that would have delighted mad King Ludwig of Bavaria, who insisted on water pouring down upon the singers in simulation of heavy rain. But complete realism in opera is impossible, for as Mozart once asked: 'Would a real thunderstorm subside during a tenor's aria?'

Accused of sailing through their roles with little attempt at acting, some prima donnas have resolved to bring as much realism as possible into their performances. After Geraldine Farrar had filmed as Carmen in five reels for Cecil B. de Mille, she returned to the Metropolitan on 17 February 1916 to play the part on its stage, and she changed her style, probably as a result of his lively direction. In Act I she slapped Caruso, her Don José, fiercely in the face, in Act II she wrestled with a cigarette factory girl, bruising and flinging her down on to the boards, and in Act III she fought Caruso like a wild cat so that the audience, arrested by these antics, took little notice of the tenor's vocal fireworks. Then, in the closing scene, she hit him hard on the jaw with her fan. In self-defence, he seized her wrist and, struggling like a captive conger to free herself, she bit his hand, drawing blood. He then hurled her from him whilst still singing his aria, so that she sat down with a bump and in that position went slithering across the stage.

At the final curtain, the audience's enthusiasm proved that they had thoroughly enjoyed such exuberance, laughter greeting Caruso when he appeared ostentatiously holding his jaw. Backstage afterwards, Farrar attacked him for having made her fall, and the stage manager had to intervene. She then shouted that if Caruso did not care for her characterization, the company could find another Carmen, to which he replied: 'No, we can prevent a repetition of these scenes by getting another Don José.'

Next day in the *New York Sun*, the eminent critic W.J. Henderson condemned 'the disillusioning vulgarity' which had marred the performance. By the time *Carmen* was presented a second time on 25 February, however, the artists were reconciled and the *New York Tribune* was able to report that Farrar 'neither slapped Don José's face nor did she maul the unhappy chorus girl'.

When *Carmen* had its première at the Opéra-Comique of Paris in 1875, Mme Galli-Marié, the first to play the title role, was accused by François Oswald, the critic, of 'over-emphasizing the seamy side of her part to such an extent that it would be difficult to go much further without incurring the intervention of the police'; whilst Léon Escudier in *L'Art Musical* considered her gestures to be 'the very incarnation of vice'.

Comettant also disapproved. In Act I, Galli-Marié became *'La Terrible Espagnole* who leaps like a tiger cat and is like a snake'. He went on:

To preserve the morale and the behaviour of the impressionable dragoons and toreadors who surround this demoiselle she should be fastened into a strait jacket after being cooled off by a jug of water poured over her head. The pathological condition of this unfortunate woman, consecrated unceasingly and pitilessly to the Fires of the Flesh, is fortunately a rare case, more likely to inspire the solicitude of physicians, than to interest decent spectators who visit the Opéra-Comique accompanied by their wives and daughters.

Tosca is another opera in the *verismo* style. When Ljuba Welitsch appeared at the Metropolitan as Floria, she complained to Lawrence Tibbett that his acting as Scarpia was not sufficiently true to life, so at the next performance he hurled her down on to the stage with such ferocity that she was too stunned to sing *'Vissi d'arte'*, with her usual brilliance. 'But I repaid him for it,' Mme Welitsch said, recalling the incident. 'As he lay on the floor pretending to be dead after I had stabbed him, I kicked him in the stomach, exactly as Tosca would have done.' She was right, of course, for Tosca, too, was a prima donna.

Callas, though she brought equal realism to her Tosca, had the grace to think of the well-being of the artist playing Scarpia. Gerald Moore in his *Farewell Recital* mentions the violence with which she stabbed her victim in the second act during a performance at Covent Garden, and says Tito Gobbi told him that when placing the candles at the head and feet of his 'corpse' she whispered: 'I hope I didn't hurt you!'

In an interview with John Mautner, published in *Opera News* for 18 March 1957, Maria Jeritza revealed how she came to sing *'Vissi d'arte'* from the prone position. Describing Puccini as the greatest *régisseur* with whom she had ever worked, she said that when they began rehearsing *Tosca* he urged: 'Look here, *carissima*. You must find something that will help this second act. It is dramatically so sound but then – poof! – I write this aria, and everything stops, and we have a conventional opera.'

'Could perhaps Scarpia . . . ,' she started suggesting, but the composer interrupted her with: 'All Scarpia can do is to look out of the window and leave Tosca to her mediation with God. *Find* something, so it won't remain an old-fashioned opera.'

It was not until the dress rehearsal that the incident occurred which was to make Jeritza's interpretation unique. Alfred Jerger, playing Scarpia, carried away by the part, threw her on to the floor with such force that she thought she had broken a rib.

To quote Jeritza's own words: 'I lay there, knowing that in a few bars I had to sing *Nur der Schönheit, weih't ich mein Leben* – the German text of *Vissi d'arte*. I didn't know how I would get back on my feet, let alone have any breath, with my entire body hurting. Then Professor Arnold Rosé, the famous first violinist of the Vienna Philharmonic, started the first bars of the aria and I just began to sing. I didn't even bother to push my dishevelled hair away from my face. When I finished, I thought to myself, "All right, now we will face the storm." But instead Puccini's voice came from the auditorium: "*Brava, brava, bella carissima!* You have *done* it. It is perfect!" '

Jeritza's triumph as Tosca in Vienna soon led to plans for a New York engagement, but the war delayed them and it was not until 1 December 1921 that she appeared in the role at the Metropolitan under the management of Gatti-Casazza, who later said that the ovation given her was the greatest he had ever heard in an opera house. Deems Taylor, critic of the *World*, recorded that she 'half fell, half slid to the floor at the celebrated moment to accomplish a vocal feat as difficult as it was effective'.

Mautner asked Jeritza if Puccini had helped her in any other way, and she replied that he had showed her how to jump to her death in Tosca by climbing on to the parapet himself and demonstrating brilliantly.

Melba's rival, Emma Calvé, was the consummate Carmen of that generation and made of her, in the words of a contemporary, 'a creature of unbridled passion, with a sensuous, suggestive grace, careless of all consequences'. When she made her début in the role at the Met in 1893, her success was such that the opera was given twelve times during the season and earned for the management over $100,000. Henry E. Krehbiel, critic of the *New York Tribune*, confessed himself to have been magnetized by the frankness of her acting, which would satisfy 'the most ardent lover of realism'.

This convincing air may help to explain the Red Sultan Abd ul Hamid's reactions when Calvé danced as well as sang before him in his palace at Constantinople. Suddenly in the middle of her performance an expression of terror came into his face and he left precipitately. She was puzzled, but a friend at the French Embassy explained; 'You probably approached too near the Sultan and it alarmed him. He lives in constant dread of being assassinated.'

'*Mon dieu!*' Calvé exclaimed. 'Surely he couldn't have been scared by my castanets or my fan?'

'Ah!' retorted the diplomat. 'Not of those, I agree – but could you not have had Carmen's dagger in your garter?'

Calvé had happier associations with another person possibly of Turkish descent, Mustafà, the penultimate *castrato* at the Sistine Chapel, thanks to whom she learned to sing with her unearthly disembodied fourth voice. He told her it would take ten years practising for two hours a day to acquire the gift, but she managed it in three.

Another Carmen who would certainly have upset the Sultan was Giulia Ravogli. Bernard Shaw wrote in his *Music in London* of her performance in the role at Covent Garden in April 1891 that it was real and that the idea of Lubert, the Spanish tenor, killing her was ridiculous. Nobody believed that she was dead – she could have picked him up and thrown him at the head of Randegger, the conductor, without exciting the least surprise 'especially among those who are good judges of conducting'. Shaw added:

Indeed, the orchestra and the front row of the stalls, delighted as they are when this wonderful Carmen is on the stage, are not altogether safe at such times. The face of Mr. Antoine Mott, the well-known trombone-player, when he realized that the knife which Carmen had just plucked from Don José's hand, and sent whizzing down the stage with a twitch of her powerful hand, was coming straight at his jugular vein, expressed a curious alloy of artistic devotion with a rueful sense that she might just as easily have aimed a little higher and made her shot at a critic instead of imperilling a brother artist.

Minnie Hauk, when rehearsing Violetta (*Traviata*), picked up and pocketed the bank-notes which the indignant Alfredo had cast at her feet. Corrected by the producer, she justified her action, saying that it was what a woman of that character would have done in real life.

It was Minnie Hauk who introduced Bizet's *Carmen* to London, and it was largely due to the fiery fashion in which she played the role that the opera had such a success.

Love-making on the stage can look ludicrous when a couple are diametrically opposite in size. David Franklin in his autobiography, *Basso Cantanto*, tells how once at Covent Garden when waiting at the side of the stage for his next entry in *Rigoletto*, he watched Edith Coates as Maddalena playing a scene with a very short tenor as the Duke. 'It was difficult to get to work on him, and she bent down, got a grip on his arms, heaved and lifted him up and set him on a table, so that she could get near enough physically for the verisimilitude of seduction.' Melba had similar trouble with Alessandro Bonci. When they first appeared together, the comic effect of their love scenes raised sniggers in the stalls. The problem was solved by her wearing low heels and Bonci elevators; thus they triumphed as Gilda and the Duke in the memorable performance of *Rigoletto* at the Met on 11 January 1907.

Some artists are able to shed copious tears when the part demands it. Elizabeth Söderstrom has that gift, but as she reveals in her autobiography *In My Own Key* she was unable to find any mascara that tears did not dissolve, causing her eyes to sting, gumming up her lids, making her nose run and resulting in her voice becoming strangled, so she learned to weep less and found it far more telling.

Convincing acting can help to hide vocal defects. Marietta Alboni was afraid of the lower F and E as her voice broke between F and G, to conceal which she tried all manner of devices. There was a passage in an opera requiring her to sing *fortissimo* on her weakest note, G: 'Away, fiend, away and never return!' Try as she might, she failed to make that note effective and to give the words the ringing emphasis they called for. At last she had an inspiration and sang instead *pianissimo*, articulating each syllable with telling clarity as she leant forward, glaring into her adversary's eyes. The effect was so terrifying that the audience burst into spontaneous applause, and she was rewarded with high praise next day from all the critics for this unexpected innovation.

Most of the examples mentioned have been of the realistic ferocity of prima donnas. Some male singers, surprisingly, have shrunk from such behaviour. Jean de Reszke disliked playing murderers and felt ill at ease as Otello and Don José. 'Naturalism is disagreeable to me,' he explained. 'To die spluttering and spitting – oh, no! It is the stage, not the hospital, where I work.'

Tito Gobbi, however, thought differently. In his fascinating autobiography *My Life* he tells how after being engaged by Serafin to sing with his company at the Teatro Reale, Rome, the young baritone had to wait four years before the maestro considered him capable of playing Posa in *Don Carlos*. As Tito studied the role it occurred to him that since this character is supposed to be shot in the back during the prison scene, in real life blood would fill his lungs and that therefore his dying phrases ought to be sung *con voce sofferente*, ending with a choking sound. So he sang in that manner at the dress rehearsal, causing Serafin to ask if he were feeling ill.

Gobbi gave his reasons for the change, but the other disapproved, insisting that the audience would want to hear him sing in full voice to the very end. After some argument, however, a compromise was reached. Tito would sing as Serafin wished at the première, but on the second night he would be allowed to experiment with his new interpretation.

For the opening, Gobbi therefore concentrated on beautiful singing throughout and received a rapturous reception. 'You see?' Serafin said afterwards. 'What did I tell you?' But the baritone contended that what mattered was how the audience reacted to the break with convention he made at the following performance. On the night, when he reached the moment where Posa is shot, Gobbi reduced the tone as if from pain and weakness, then choked, and no sooner was his body still, as if in death, than the whole house rose and cheered, completely captivated by such telling realism.

After the performance, Serafin made the *amende honorable*. He brought the opera house's managing director and the Mayor of Rome to Tito Gobbi's dressing-room and told him he had done so because he wanted them to witness what he had to say. 'Tonight I discovered that even an old man can sometimes learn from a young one. You are right, Tito. Go on in your own way.' And that, said Gobbi, was his first step towards a new kind of realism in opera.

He is, of course, a superb actor. The trouble is that many singers are unable to act really convincingly however much they try. Frank Corsaro, the American operatic director, once cynically remarked: 'If you want a tenor to look as if he is thinking let him walk down a flight of stairs.' Of Melba, Percy Colson wrote:

She was never able to call up a look of tragedy more intense than that of the lady who has forgotten the name of the gentlemen who is taking her out to supper and does not want to hurt his feelings. . . . Her acting never got much beyond the rudimentary stage. To express a mild emotion, such as Juliet's love for Romeo, she would raise one arm. To express extreme passion or violent despair, she would raise two.

During rehearsals at the Metropolitan, whenever a soprano holding on to a high C stretched out an arm with palm upward, Toscanini would try and cure her from making that stock gesture by asking: 'Is it raining?'

In *The Sunday Times* for 22 July 1951 Ernest Newman claimed that these simple gestures are common to most singers:

Whenever I turn over the pages on Indian or some other oriental art and see some god or hero in swaggering possession of four or six arms I cannot help regretting that opera singers have not been constructed on similarly generous lines. Think of how many permutations and combinations even four arms would be capable! They would make all kinds of psychological subtleties and contrarieties possible – as it were a counterpoint of gesture.

Newman reminded his readers of the story of Gluck's correction of the hasty critic who objected that it was absurd to make Orestes sing 'Now calm possesses my heart again' to an agitated orchestral accompaniment. Gluck explained that Orestes was actually lying as he had murdered his mother and the orchestra was contradicting him. Newman suggested that if the player of Orestes had had an extra pair of arms there might have been no misunderstanding on the critic's part, for the cross-currents in the hero's soul would have been made perfectly clear by cross-rhythms of the arms.

With such an equipment, again, Otello, by a convulsive movement of the north-east arm, might convey to us that he was revengefully bent on murdering Desdemona, while by a counterpoint in a contrary rhythm in the south-west arm he could convince us that he still had a soft spot in his heart for the poor girl and very much regretted having to be so tough with her.

Another operatic situation in which Newman thought mixed emotions could best be conveyed to an audience by four arms occurs in *Don Giovanni* at the point when Zerlina cannot make up her mind whether or not to yield to 'the Don's smooth suggestion that she will allow him to entertain her at his villa, and show her his stamp collection'.

And then, when the ramparts are down and the fortress is taken partly by storm, partly through treachery within the gates, and she and Giovanni unite in a cry of 'Come on, come on, my hawk, my pigeon, let us make up for lost time' . . . I translate psychologically rather than verbally – what shifting nuances of the eternal subject and counter-subject of the *Ewig-weibliche* and the *Ewig-mannliche* could be expressed by a sort of eight-part Bachian counterpoint of arms! But, alas, opera singers, like the rest of us, are restricted to two.

However, as the *Daily Mail* critic wrote of Montserrat Caballé as Leonora in *Il trovatore* at Covent Garden in the late 1970s, what matters most is the quality of the singing, and one must overlook, as in this diva's case, 'the constant flow of arm movements that obviously need to be seen at their best with a line of traffic behind her'. And when it comes to recitals on the concert platform, there are those in an audience who would prefer no gesticulating at all, as well as those easy-going escapists who would wholeheartedly endorse Sir Henry Wood's instructions to singers: 'Smile! Smile! Even when you are singing of death –smile!'

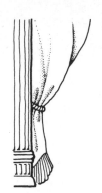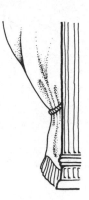

Lighting

Lighting can make a diva look happy when singing of death even if a recent face-lift inhibits her from smiling. Prima donnas have often kept close control over stage lighting. Maria Jeritza would insist that it be changed to match her dress, both in the opera house and in the concert hall. Gerald Moore in *Am I Too Loud?* says that Melba during her last tour of America would test lighting effects after a recital had begun, while her supporting musicians were performing. When Beatrice Harrison opened with a group of violoncello solos, she had to endure lights being raised and lowered, and spots and foots flashed on until Dame Nellie was satisfied with the results.

Beverley Nichols relates how when touring her own company in Australia, Melba, during the rehearsals for Verdi's *Otello*, after satisfying herself that the crimson curtains round Desdemona's bed were arranged to her liking, shouted to the electricians: 'More yellow, more yellow – this isn't a surgery! You're blinding me! That's better. Wait a minute – not so much of that spotlight on the bed. I'm not a music-hall artist!' Then she added in an undertone; 'How does that man think Desdemona could go to sleep with a light like that glaring in her eyes?'

Male stars, too, can be difficult over lighting. At the Metropolitan, Jussi Björling, when young, once played the title role in *Faust* to Chaliapin's Mephistopheles. The Russian focused the audience's attention on himself not only through his fine acting but also through his having bribed the electrician to keep the spotlight solely on himself. In the opening scene, when Mephistopheles appears to offer Faust eternal youth, the huge figure of the bass was draped in a voluminous red cape which with

95

a grand gesture he spread over Björling, thus forcing him to sing for the rest of the act cut off from the sight of both audience and conductor.

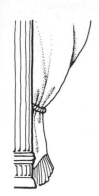
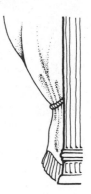

The Trill

A prima donna should, of course, see that a spotlight is on her when she is engaged in something vocally difficult at which she excels, such as trilling. Joseph Wechsberg in his book *The Opera* has written that *coloratura* prima donnas are 'better remembered for vocal trills and thrills than musicianship'. As a young boy he first heard in Vienna Selma Kurz in *Rigoletto* and says with admiration that he will never forget her trill at the end of *'Caro nome'*, which seemed to last for ages as she slowly walked off the stage. Later, when he joined the claque, he used to time the trill with a stop-watch. 'Once it lasted a record 21 seconds, which I now realize was not only a record of vocal bravura but also of vocal taste.'

Hector Berlioz was not so enthusiastic. In *Les Grotesques de la musique* he states that one evening, after a prima donna had ' just succeeded in bursting our ear drums, an amateur asked him, 'What do you think of the vocal trill?'

The composer claims that he replied:

The vocal trill can sometimes be very effective, as an expression of innocent pleasure, or as an imitation of graceful laughter, but when employed without any reason, when introduced into serious music, and into every bar at that, it gets on my nerves: it drives me mad. This reminds me of the cruelties which, as a youth, I used to inflict upon our unfortunate cockerels. I was then almost as much exasperated by the triumphant cry of a cock as I am now pained by the victorious trill of a prima donna. Many a time have I laid in ambush waiting for the sultan bird to start up its ridiculous screech (some people call it a song!) to an accompaniment of much flapping of wings, for the pleasure of promptly interrupting him and frequently stunning him with a stone. . . .

Also, the vocal trill is usually stupid in itself, and as vile and absurd as the shakes, slides and other disgraces with which Lully and his like so liberally decorated their wretched melodies. When executed on a high note by certain sopranos it becomes a wild animal (like the listener), for the destruction of which a hundred-and-ten pounder would not be too great.

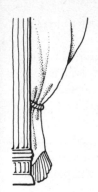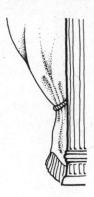

Encores

For those whose heaven on earth is an opera house, the longer they can remain there the better, and they must envy the good fortune of Emperor Franz Josef, the only man for whom the whole of an opera was repeated as an encore. This occurred when Cimarosa's *Il matrimonio segreto* was performed in Vienna before him. *'Bravo, bravissimo!'* he complimented the composer. 'It is admirable, delightful, enchanting! I did not applaud that I might not miss a single note of this masterpiece. You have heard it twice and I must have the same pleasure before I go to bed.'

Many, however, have regarded encores as a nuisance. Of the early divas Angelica Catalani was a notorious offender at the beginning of the nineteenth century, and her example was followed by other singers at Covent Garden until at last the management issued the following notice: 'Whereas by the frequent calling for the songs again, the Operas have been too tedious, therefore the singers are forbidden to sing any song above once.'

Patti never tired of giving encores. In April 1892, when she ended one of her farewell tours of the United States with an afternoon concert at the Metropolitan, it was said that never had she sung so much at one performance before. When the audience refused to leave, she had the piano moved in front of the curtain, and with her secretary as accompanist sang whatever was called for.

Maria Malibran at the start of her career played Desdemona in Rossini's *Otello*. Discovering that she refused to sing again once her father, in the role of the Moor, had stabbed her to death, the audience, when he was about to do so, would hold up the action

99

with their cries of 'Home, Sweet Home', forcing her to sing this before Garcia killed her.

Melba, taking the same part in Verdi's *Otello* (in which Desdemona is strangled), would, if the applause were loud enough, come back to life at the end, ordering stagehands to wheel a piano centre-stage, and would sing Bishop's popular song to her own accompaniment.

Emma Eames and Marcella Sembrich would deliberately incite audiences to demand repetition of the Letter Scene in *Le nozze di Figaro*, by pretending that the ink had spilled over the paper and that the letter must be rewritten.

In its issue for 1 June 1923, the *Musical Times* complained:

The depths to which famous singers have sunk in this matter of encores is shown by the fact that last year, when the Northcliffe Press boosted Melba's Albert Hall concert, we were told beforehand what the encores were to be. 'For encores I shall sing so and so . . . .' That a singer should be prepared is right, and considerate to the accompanist, but this calm announcement days beforehand is the last word in assurance. Only divas seem to be so blessed with a forehead of brass.

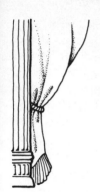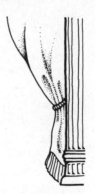

Applause

The feast of song is now finished. It is up to us to let the artists know what we thought of it all. In ancient India audiences would snap the fingers on one hand after a mediocre performance and those of both hands in recognition of brilliance. In provincial France they stamp their feet, whilst in Spain some opera buffs hiss to express admiration.

A. B. Walkley, the famous critic of *The Times*, disapproved of clapping and once wrote: 'If you think of it, striking one palm against the other with a resounding smack is a queer way of expressing your delight; it suggests a monkey trick of primaeval man.'

Ernest Newman wished that audiences would not applaud at all and, instead, 'go out in rapt silence after a great performance of a great work'. Neither did he care for the custom at concerts of greeting popular artists with applause before they performed.

George R. Marek, in *Opera News* for 18 December 1971, wrote amusingly about how an experienced singer can induce or milk applause and described some of the most effective ways of doing this. The simplest method was to take one step forward on the last note of the aria, with head well back, the eyes raised towards the 'Family Circle' and the arms flung up as if to embrace the chandelier. Then there were those who pressed the back of a hand against the brow, with head drooping forward – known as the 'take-my-temperature' ending. The 'monument stance' consisted of remaining completely motionless the moment the clapping commenced, then when it starts to subside, the artist immediately bows down almost to the boards as if overcome with emotion. A variation was the 'I don't deserve it' attitude, expressed by shrugging, with palms turned towards the audience protesting one's unworthiness to be so acclaimed. When an act ended, the 'shot-from-a-cannon' trick was to be recommended: the singer lingers behind the curtain as long as intuition advises, then runs in front of it. The 'Gaston-Alphonse' ruse was a method of scoring off another artist when you shared a curtain call. With a show of modesty you pressed him to precede you backstage, using a little propulsion if necessary. This enable you to stay a few seconds longer before your public.

The order of appearance for solo calls has led to arguments and disputes, the most prestigious position being at the end of the queue of those awaiting acclamation. During the rule of Sir Rudolf Bing at the Met, he had displayed in the dressing-rooms his instructions as to precedence for every opera, and no deviation was allowed. The principle guiding him when drawing these up was the importance of the role and not that of the singer.

Eric Blom in his 'Essay on Performing and Listening' wrote that in his experience whenever British audiences went to extremes over showing their enthusiasm at musical performances, it was often after an artist had committed some appalling mistake, too conspicuous to pass unnoticed by even the least sensitive ear. This was due to a misguided spirit of sportsmanship that expressed itself on such occasions with an intensity that was 'humanly touching, but both ludicrous and exasperating from an aesthetic point of view'.

Probably the performer with the greatest passion for plaudits was Patti. Bernard Shaw wrote that she would get up and bow to one in the very agony of stage death even if one only dropped one's stick accidentally.

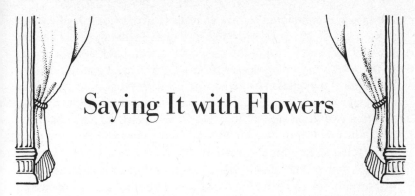

Saying It with Flowers

Applause is not enough. The singers must have something more tangible as tokens of appreciation. In ancient Rome, approving audiences pelted popular actresses with bracelets and other heavy jewellery. By the time opera became established as a form of entertainment a change to bouquets had taken place, though some admirers showed more originality – such as the miners of America's Wild West who flung gold and silver nuggets at their favourite songbirds; or the admirer of Callas who, according to Sir Rudolf Bing, threw her a bunch of radishes after a matinée at the Met, which, being short-sighted, she mistook for tea roses.

But even floral tributes can cause a prima donna to wish she were wearing a visor, especially if thorny roses hit her face. Nowadays, at least, they would usually be cellophane-wrapped. One Victorian prided himself on being able to bowl a bouquet right on target from the back row of the pit at Covent Garden. Nevertheless, despite such hazards, these trophies were highly prized. When Maria Malibran took her benefit at the Théâtre des Italiens in Paris on 31 March 1830, an avalanche of flowers rained upon her during the final scene. As, in the role of Desdemona, she lay on the stage watching Otello prepare to commit suicide, he heard her whisper fiercely: 'Mind where you fall – don't crush any of my flowers.'

One may wonder what happened to all these bouquets. According to Henry Sutherland Edwards, the Victorian critic, the prima donna would either distribute them among friends who had come to congratulate her at the end of the performance or, selecting two or three of the most beautiful, give the rest to her maid who would then sell them to a florist. 'At a café concert to

103

offer a singer a bouquet is only another way of presenting her with a few francs,' he goes on. 'The bouquet is handed to her, not thrown, and at the end of the concert is taken back at a reduction by the accommodating dealer from whom it has been purchased. But small things must not be compared with great, nor the doings of a singer at a café concert with those of an operatic prima donna.'

When two divas appear together in an opera, disputes over the horticultural offerings can arise. At Chicago in 1884 Adelina Patti and Etelka Gerster performed in Meyerbeer's *Les Huguenots*, but, through an attendant's mistake, several large bouquets meant for presentation to Patti after the second and third acts were passed to her at the end of the first, when Valentine, the part she was playing, hardly sings at all and Gerster, as the Queen, had taken full advantage of her many opportunities to impress. As a result of the Hungarian soprano being thus unrewarded, the spectators stopped applauding Patti, and when at last a tiny bunch of flowers was given to Gerster they made up for her lack of blooms with tumultuous clapping. This contretemps so vexed Patti that, when the opera was over, she became hysterical and accused impresario Colonel Mapleson of plotting to make her unpopular with the public so that he could reduce the fees paid her.

Having begun her spectacular career at the age of 7 as 'The Wonderful Child Prima Donna', Adelina soon became blasé about bouquets and even sniffed at gold laurel crowns. Louis Engel once informed her that money was being raised by admirers so as to give her one. 'What, another!' she cried. 'That's the forty-third. Please tell them I'd much rather have a diamond bracelet. Why, the Jockey Club in Paris presented me with twelve crowns the same evening as if I had twelve heads to wear them all!'

Minnie Hauk is generally believed to have been the first Carmen in America, but Clara Louise Kellogg, in her *Memoirs*, claimed that distinction for herself. She also wrote that when they both appeared in Meyerbeer's *The Star of the North*, Minnie, who was 'very pushing', used to help Clara to collect her bouquets.

The only trouble was that every one she picked up, she kept! As a rule I did not object, and, anyway, I might have had difficulty in proving that she had appropriated my flowers after she had taken the cards off; but one night she included in her general haul a bouquet from a young man who always sent the same kind of flowers. I recognized it, saw her take it, but, as there was no card, had the greatest difficulty in getting it away from her. I did, though, in the end.

Malibran and Henriette Sontag were rivals, too, and one night at the Paris Opéra a floral wreath fell close to the former. Thinking it was intended for her, she was about to grasp it when a stern voice from the pit shouted: 'Leave that alone – it isn't for you!' To which Malibran scornfully retorted: 'I would not deprive Mlle Sontag of the wreath – I'd rather place one on her.'

Friends often applaud even before the singer utters a sound. On one occasion in Mapleson's experience when a soprano appeared in *Il trovatore* about a dozen bouquets fell at her feet from the top boxes before she had sung a note.

George Bernard Shaw disapproved of floral tributes. After attending a performance by students of the Royal College of Music at the Prince of Wales's Theatre in July 1889, he regretted that 'the bad custom of bouquet-throwing' was permitted and added in his review that an American prima donna was the offender. 'What do you mean, Madame Nordica, by teaching the young idea how to get bouquets shied? One consolation is that if the critics cannot control the stars, they can at least administer the stripes.'

Six weeks later, after listening to 'an American lady whistler' at Her Majesty's, he wrote:

She travels with enormous wreaths and baskets of flowers, which are handed to her at the conclusion of her pieces. And no matter how often this happens, she is never a whit the less astonished to see the flowers come up. . . . Nobody except the very greenest of greenhorns is taken in. . . . Some day I shall get up an affiliated Society of Hissers and Hooters, whose mission it will be to attend first appearances in force and hiss all bogus demonstrations until the sight of a basket of flowers becomes more dreadful to a débutante than any fear of a cold reception could possibly be.

But the bouquet tradition was too deeply rooted to be felled by even so powerful a critic's blast. Thirty-two years further on, an editorial in the *Musical Times* for August 1921 claimed: 'The bouquet business is largely engineered. We have seen débutantes smothered with floral tributes after a medioc1 ᵉ performance of their first song. When half-baked artists compound this sort of felony, it is time for the really big singers and players to return to simplicity.' Then, proceeding to commend Paderewski's refusal to accept a wreath at a recent recital, the writer declared:

There is point in a wreath that may be worn on the head, the place where the wreath ought to go, but an affair like a cart-wheel suggests either a head abnormally swollen (even for a soloist) or use as a girdle for a 20 in. waist. We have seen musicians – among others Stravinsky – solemnly standing on the platform holding such a wreath. Only two, in our experience, have realized the absurdity of the thing, and risen to the occasion. Both were pianists: Pachmann grinned through the wreath, as through a horse-collar; Paderewski ignored it, and the cart-wheel of greenery was borne off ingloriously by an attendant.

The editor of the *Musical Times* might have added the names of Sir Thomas Beecham and Toscanini to those mentioned as rising to the occasion. When presented with a large wreath after the first performance of his *The Gods Go A-Begging* by the Russian Ballet, the former nonchalantly left the stage bowling it like a child's hoop, whilst Toscanini, when offered one, waved it aside, saying: 'They are for prima donnas or corpses – I am neither.'

Today, however, the mounting cost of salvoes of bouquets has drastically reduced their numbers and no one will begrudge a prima donna the few she can expect to receive on a special occasion. It is unlikely that any diva could now claim as Melba once did: 'If I had only the money that has been spent in flowers for me and nothing else, I should be a very rich woman.'

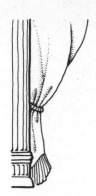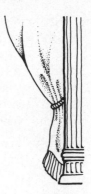

The Claque

Audiences can be more deserving of criticism than the performers and yet critics seldom mention their shortcomings. The need to stimulate applause when the listeners fail to respond as they should led to the claque coming into being. Joseph Schostal, chief of the celebrated claque in the fourth gallery of the Staatsoper in Vienna, used to say: 'The claque makes opera grand.' In his book *Red Plush and Black Velvet*, Joseph Wechsberg says he spent the best years of his opera life as a member of this 'highly exclusive group of deeply dedicated opera lovers, whose musical refinement was not always matched by their financial solvency. By way of using the former to achieve the latter, the claque members would receive free tickets from the claque chief, in return for which they would clap their hands at the right moment for the right person in the right manner, a feat far more difficult to achieve than most opera-goers would imagine.'

Schostal was a man of high principles whose dictum was: 'Applause must be earned.' Mr Wechsberg stresses that even though he accepted money from artists, he made it clear that he was under no moral obligation to deliver applause unless it was deserved. He wrote:

He might decide during the aria of one of our clients that the singer wasn't good enough that night. . . . Schostal would slowly shake his large bald head . . . and the members of the claque, scattered all over the gallery, would know that the order had been rescinded. Or it might happen that a singer who hadn't paid Schostal a single schilling suddenly electrified the audience with an unexpected display of vocal fireworks. Schostal would not hesitate to bestow upon him a deserved tribute, free of charge.

He would attend rehearsals, make notes in his score, study reports from his secret intelligence network inside the Staatsoper, then a quarter of an hour before curtain up Schostal would stand near a marble column in the downstairs lobby, handing out tickets and instructions. Each *claqueur* received one ticket and nothing else. Wechsberg insists that insinuations that they were paid to applaud were false and mostly spread by a rival clique operated downstairs by one Stieglitz, who was more impressed by the financial contributions of his clients than by their vocal achievements.

On important evenings when Maria Jeritza sang against Alfred Piccaver, or Leo Slezak against Lotte Lehmann, Schostal would summon the suicide squads of the claque, called *Hohlposcher*, courageous *condottieri* able to produce that special, dark, sepulchral sound which had the supreme professional finish . . . . When the *Hohlposcher* clapped their hands, you thought a tank regiment was rumbling by at high speed over an old, cobblestoned street.

In the middle 1920s the Schostal claque supported Mme Lehmann while the Stieglitz clique were employed by Mme Jeritza, and there were many exciting evenings in Vienna's opera house, such as a memorable performance of *Der Rosenkavalier* with the former as the Marschallin and the latter as Octavian. As the curtain rose, Jeritza sat at one end of her couch while Lehmann crouched at the other. 'Despite the orgiastic music of the Prelude it was very hard to realize that the Marschallin and Octavian had supposedly just spent a passionate night,' writes Joseph Wechsberg. 'Throughout their scenes the two divas outmanoeuvred each other skilfully, under the watchful eyes of Richard Strauss, composer, conductor and referee of the opera. At the end of each act there were wild outbursts of uncontrollable enthusiasm, in which even the plain-clothes men took part.' The tumult after the final curtain led to the entire membership present of both the claque and the clique being arrested and marched off to the police station.

It is said that guests in the nearby Hotel Sacher hastily paid their bills and left, thinking revolution had broken out. Wechsberg remarks that *Der Rosenkavalier* was an impossible opera from the claque's point of view, as there are no arias and applause was permitted only at the end of each act. They knew that the clique downstairs would try to clap and shout louder than they did, so Schostal briefed them: 'Tonight it is our mission to produce volume. Men, the honour of our institution is at stake.'

'All divas have invisible audiometers built in to their competitive hearing systems,' writes Wechsberg. 'They know at once whether the rival's applause is a few decibels louder or softer than their own – and God help you if theirs is softer.'

Your *primo uomo*, too, is often just as eager for noisy acclamation. Caruso found it an essential stimulant and bought tickets for on average seventy friends and fans to attend his performances.

He would also personally inspect the box-office's plans to ensure that the seats were systematically distributed so that his claque, through their lead, might rouse all parts of the house to render appropriate homage to his vocal genius.

To ensure Christine Nilsson's success when she made her début in London at Her Majesty's in 1867, Mapleson engaged some twenty-four horny-handed Thames watermen who were told that when the first act was over and the curtain had fallen, they would be paid a shilling each for every time they could get it up again with their clapping.

Reports vary as to how many curtains were thus obtained. Some say six, others ten. The impresario wrote: 'That was all that was ever done for Mlle Nilsson. Her extraordinary talent did the rest. At all events it gave her a fair start and her début was the talk of London.'

According to Mapleson, in Victorian times there was an unwritten law that all prima donnas had the right to a number of free seats in the various parts of the opera houses in which they sang. The purpose of this was so that their friends could start and whip up the appreciative clamour.

There were many prominent vocalists who took with them on tours abroad a *chef de claque*. If one popular tenor travelled with a staff of eight, his rival following him to the same country would make a point of taking with him one of nine, so that the fact might be mentioned in the press and increase his prestige. Mapleson wrote:

A certain tenor went not long since to South America with a staff consisting of the following paid officials: a secretary, an undersecretary, a cook, a valet, a barber, a doctor, a lawyer, a journalist, an agent and a treasurer. The ten attendants, apart from their special duties, form a useful claque, and are kept judiciously distributed about the house according to their social position.

It was said that they squabbled at times over who should have to sit in the gallery and who in a box, and so on.

The lawyer's official duties were to draw up contracts and to claim damages from the impresario immediately the requirements of any clause were breached in the slightest way. 'The hire of all these attendants', wrote Mapleson, 'causes no perceptible hole in the immense salary payable to the artist who employs them; and the travelling expenses of a good number of them have to be defrayed by the unfortunate manager.'

Hector Berlioz in his *Evenings with the Orchestra* wrote with entertaining irony about *claqueurs*. He points out that it was Nero who first hired men to applaud him when he sang in public. According to the composer, there are several ways of acclaiming an artist. The amateur hits one hand against the other, producing a dull, commonplace sound, but the professional strikes the fingers of his right hand in the hollow of his left, thus obtaining a sharp, resonant report that is far more effective.

As he does so, the *claqueur* looks left and right and if those around him are not following his example he shouts: *'Bravo-o-o-o! Bravo-o-o-o!'* or *'Brava!'* And as the cloud of dust arising through his stamping thickens, his cheering grows louder.

Berlioz wrote:

The violinist-*claqueur* strikes the body of his instrument with the back of his bow. This form of admiration, rarer than the rest, has more distinction. Unfortunately disillusioning experience has taught prima donnas that it is difficult to know whether such plaudits are ironical or genuine. Hence the uneasy smiles when such homage is paid them.

The kettledrummer shows his approval by hitting his drums, but this does not happen once in fifteen years.

Then there is the sensitive female *claqueur*, who goes into noisy hysterics and faints. A rare species and very closely related to the giraffe family.

Berlioz describes how and on what terms the professionals work. The claque chieftain, concealed in a box, attends all the artists' rehearsals prior to briefing his own troupe of hirelings, and decides where to clap and on how many rounds of it and where to shout 'Encore!'.

The existence of the claque, continues the composer, had influenced his own profession, causing some of his confrères to end pieces with the *cabaletta* which always incited audiences to applaud. Those no longer satisfied with the effect produced by this had introduced the big drum into the orchestra.

To banish the claque from the Paris Opéra seemed unthinkable to Berlioz.

Can one imagine the depths of despondency into which all the singers and musicians would sink; the disgust with life, the thoughts of suicide that would take possession of the operatic deities when a *cabaletta* sung in less than faultless style is succeeded by an ominous hush? Just envisage the fury of mediocre artistes on seeing real talent only applauded, whilst they themselves get not a single clap? . . . Who would cover up with tactful applause the false note of a bass or tenor, and so prevent the public from hearing it? The very thought makes one shudder. Furthermore to watch the claque at work adds to the appeal of the show; it is a joy to see it in full cry. This is so true that were the *claqueurs* refused admission to certain performances, there would not be a soul in the house.

Berlioz lists some of the principal duties of the claque – to applaud artists on appearance even before they open their mouths; to pursue them with plaudits as they go off into the wings, no matter what they last said or did; to sing their praises in the passages, foyer and bars. He mentions some of the signals given by the leader to his followers. If he uttered 'Brrrr!' it meant 'Clap till your hands ache and stamp your feet', whilst a smile as he swayed his head from side to side called for moderate laughter. A sudden burst of it should explode immediately he slapped his uplifted hands fiercely together: when they remained raised longer than usual, then the laughter must be prolonged and followed by a round of applause. A mournful 'Hum!', on the other hand, meant express sorrow by blowing your noses noisily.

Jan Pierce in *The Blue Bird of Happiness* called Grace Moore 'the first lady of claquery'. He alleged that she enlisted as her *claqueurs* only those who could cheer and clap the loudest, and with aim so accurate that they never failed to make the posies of violets she loved fall at her feet. As Pierce, night after night, bent down, picked up a few and handed them to her, she would smile at him and always say: 'I wish I knew who's doing that!'

Pierce comments that he knew all the flowers were returned later to her unknown admirers, but restrained himself from telling her so. Once, however, he could not resist replying with an amiable smile: 'Just look at your payroll at the end of the month.'

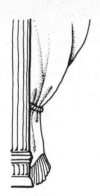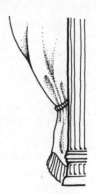

'Cash-Cash!'

Floral and other tributes, and loyal claques – what else does a Queen of Song need? Certainly earnings must be sufficient for her to live in the style proper to that exalted station. This has made her open her mouth wider than usual at times. When he heard the fee Maria Callas was asking to sing at the Metropolitan, Sir Rudolf Bing exclaimed: 'Why, even the President of the United States doesn't receive so much in one year.' To which she retorted: 'Then let him sing for you.'

In arguments over terms, the prima donna normally has the last word. Birgit Nilsson was discussing a new contract for appearing at the Vienna Opera when she pulled too hard in excitement at her necklace and it snapped, strewing all the pearls over the floor. Herbert von Karajan and his assistants got down on their knees to hunt for them. 'We mustn't miss one,' he cried. 'These are the expensive pearls Miss Nilsson buys with the high fees she gets from the Met!' 'Oh, no!' she contradicted. 'These are only imitations that I buy with my low fees from the Vienna Opera!'

Garry O'Connor wrote in his biography of Maggie Teyte, *The Pursuit of Perfection*, that even in later life she would walk up and down her room repeating out loud: 'Money, money, money – I must have money.'

Mapleson in his memoirs says of Patti: 'No one ever approached her in the art of obtaining from a manager the greatest sum he could by any possibility continue to pay.' The parrot which was her companion when she toured America had been taught by Nicolini, her second husband, to cry 'Cash! Cash!' whenever the impresario appeared.

Mapleson states that he learnt from long experience that there were only two ways of judging opera singers: first, by their artistic merit, and second, by the effect of their singing on the receipts. He would begin with the former yardstick, but once a singer had appeared before an audience he was forced by financial realities to resort to the second, and calculate whether the amount of money drawn by the artist was enough to justify the cost of his or her services. The latter, Mapleson points out, was the favourite system of Domenico Barbaja, the illiterate former dishwasher and most ferocious of impresarios, who controlled La Scala and later the San Carlo in the first half of the nineteenth century and who, when asked his private opinion of a vocalist, would reply: 'I have not yet consulted my books. I must see what the receipts were, and I will answer your question tomorrow.'

Harry Higgins, who managed Covent Garden in Edwardian times, was so staggered by the extortionate demands of a sexually-attractive Italian diva that he told her: 'My dear lady, I only want you to *sing*.'

Giulio Gatti-Casazza at the Metropolitan used to keep two sets of books: one he showed to singers who requested a rise; the other he produced only for inspection by his board of directors to reassure them the opera house was solvent.

Not all prima donnas place money first. When Mapleson held his second season of Italian opera at the Lyceum in 1862, his rival, Frederick Gye of Covent Garden, sent his manager to Thérèse Tietjens with a contract already signed by Gye, leaving blank the amount to be paid her. She was to fill in any figure she chose. It was a trying moment and her family urged her to take advantage of this unique offer. Tietjens, however, replied: 'I have given my word to Colonel Mapleson to sing for him, which is better than all contracts.'

Mapleson also found Giulia Grisi most amenable. When separated from her first husband, it was stipulated that he was to be paid £2,000 a year out of her earnings, which left her with very little on which to live. So the impresario made an agreement with her by which she was to sing for nothing on his tours whilst he paid £300 to the great tenor, Mario, who accompanied her and whom she later married. Mapleson wrote that in return they were ready to sing as often as he liked.

Like many rich people, Melba was mean in paltry matters.

Beverley Nichols, who was her secretary, says she disliked spending money on telegrams and would devote much time trying to delete unnecessary words, with the result that often her message could not be understood by the person receiving it, who would then have to wire back asking what she meant. One day she decided to use in future the phrase 'Touched thought' as an abbreviation for 'Touched by your thought'. This led to an unfortunate incident. A letter arrived from an Australian woman visiting London in which she invited Melba to dinner that evening. Accompanying the letter was a huge basket full of costly yellow orchids.

'I certainly shan't dine with her,' Melba told Nichols. 'She's one of the people who say I drink. Send her a telegram – "Regret indisposed".'

He asked if she ought not to be thanked for the orchids. Melba snorted. 'You can add "Touched thought". It'll all come into twelve words.' And that was the message sent over the phone.

Unfortunately the operator must have been hard of hearing, for the telegram delivered to the woman responsible for the rumour that Melba was an alcoholic read: 'REGRET INDISPOSED. TOUCHED PORT.' The recipient dined out on it for weeks.

Francesco Tamagno was reputed to have the most powerful voice of his times and his highest notes rattled the chandeliers at Covent Garden. Although he was paid enormous fees, he was also extremely mean.

Once, after dessert at a dinner in New York, he took from his pocket a bag and proceeded to fill it with almonds, chocolates and some orchids from the table, explaining to the wife of the Italian Ambassador that his daughter was ill and that he wished to take her a little gift.

Some days later Melba and Tamagno were invited by Maestro Luigi Mancinelli to lunch in a restaurant. After the main dish the tenor obtained a newspaper from the waiter and wrapped up the veal cutlet remaining on the prima donna's plate, saying: 'My dog he love *cotoletta alla Milanese.*'

Next morning Mancinelli called unexpectedly on Tamagno at his hotel. It was twelve o'clock and the singer and his wife and daughter were eating a sort of picnic lunch in their bedroom. That evening the maestro told Melba: 'And as you may have already guessed, they were feasting on your *cotoletta alla Milanese.*'

115

The Elephant that Swallowed a Nightingale

Dr Johnson's famous saying that only a fool does not write for money has also been applicable to some composers. When Igor Stravinsky was offered $4,000 to compose the music for a film, he answered that it was not enough. The Hollywood producer pointed out that that was the sum they had paid another renowned composer for working on their previous opus. To this Stravinsky retorted: 'He had talent. I have not, so for me the work is more difficult.' After a substantially larger sum had been agreed, the producer told a colleague: 'Now I've learnt the musical scale begins and ends with dough.'

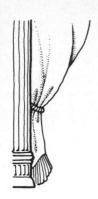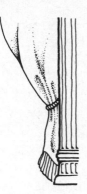

Fan Worship

The word 'diva' means, of course, goddess, and worshippers showed their adoration both by pouring their votive offerings into the box-office and by their excessively frenzied behaviour. The wild scenes caused by fans desperate to obtain access to 'rock' concerts, and the idolizing of film stars in Hollywood's heyday are by no means a phenomenon of modern times.

In the last century young men would unharness the horses from their favourite singer's carriage and pull it themselves from the opera house to her home or hotel. The students of Göttingen, after paying this homage to Henriette Sontag, threw her coach into the river so that no one could ever desecrate the vehicle.

Jenny Lind's début in 1847 at Her Majesty's Theatre, London, saw thousands of sightseers blocking the Haymarket for hours, and ticket-holders struggling to obtain admission found their finery, in the words of *The Times*, 'reduced to rags', whilst ladies fainted in the pressure and 'even gentlemen were carried out senseless'.

Thrice sittings of the House of Commons had to be suspended because most MPs were absent listening to the 'Swedish Nightingale'. Shopkeepers found that merchandise sold far more readily and at inflated prices if named after the new idol, who aroused admiration in the most unlikely people, such as the London hangman whose appreciative remark after attending a performance was: 'What a throat to scrag!'

In the United States the Jenny Lind fever became an epidemic, and trade was brisk with everything from 'Jenny Lind' bonnets to singing kettles. A wily fellow displayed a glove he claimed to be hers, and charged for kissing it – more for the inside than for the outside.

The next diva to excite similar enthusiasm was Patti. Take this description in the *Morning Call* for 15 March 1884, of the turbulence outside the box-office of the Grand Opera House, San Francisco, when thousands fought to buy tickets to hear her sing:

A line began to form as early as five o'clock in the morning, and it grew and multiplied until at ten o'clock it had turned the corner on Third Street, while the main entrance was packed solid with a writhing and twisting mass of humanity, pressed close to the glass doors . . . guarded by a lone policeman. He did his best to reduce the pressure upon himself and upon them, but as the time passed and the box-office did not open, the crowd became more noisy and unmanageable, and finally an irresistible rush was made for the doors . . . .

In the fierce tumult which followed the glass was all broken, a boy being hurled bodily through one of the panes. . . . The potted plants were overturned and annihilated under the feet of the throng. . . . A great struggle ensued to get as near as possible to the box-office. . . . The more powerful forced themselves to the front and started a new line without any regard for those who had been first in position before the barriers were overturned. . . . The air was thick and sultry, the crowd perspired and blasphemed, and the storming of the box-office became imminent. Just at this juncture Captain Short arrived with a large squad of police . . . and the crowd sullenly fell back . . . .

There was a more peaceful demonstration of mass monomania when Tetrazzini sang for charity at an open-air concert held on Christmas Eve, 1910, from a platform in the centre of San Francisco. A quarter of a million people packed the streets and, although she used no microphone, some standing half a mile away claimed they heard every word, and the cheering even reached those on ships out at sea.

Nowadays, or course, 'pop' groups draw the multitudes, but though the numbers attracted by operatic stars may be fewer, their adulation can be just as intense. When Emma Calvé visited Honolulu at the end of last century, her boat was welcomed by hundreds of balloons with her picture attached to each one, blown out from the harbour, and three hundred cowboys with banners awaited her landing.

Tito Gobbi played Scarpia when in January 1964 the finest singing actress of modern times made her triumphant return to Covent Garden as Tosca. Strict instructions were issued that nobody except members of the company was allowed to attend rehearsals. Gobbi relates how, when a cold caused Callas to be absent on one occasion, John Copley took her place.

That day a well-known titled lady visited the box-office to collect her tickets and, aware that the artists were rehearsing, entreated Sergeant Martin to open the door a fraction so that she could get a glimpse of the soprano. Receiving a firm but tactful refusal, Lady X tried again. Could he at least for a second or two open the little window into the auditorium so that she might hear Mme Callas singing?

The Sergeant decided that there could be no harm in permitting this good friend of Covent Garden such a small favour. It so happened that just as he did as requested, bearded, bespectacled John Copley, lying in Gobbi's arms, screamed: '*Ah più non posso, ah che orror!*'

'Ah, the unmistakable voice!' murmured the entranced listener, and after thanking Sergeant Martin profusely she left happily.

Composers, too, have had their share of fan worship, though on a lesser scale, and sometimes it has been in a strange form. In the latter days of the Third Empire a story went round the salons in Paris about a Countess who was infatuated with Gounod and who called on him whilst his family were away. Passing through the dining-room where the composer had just finished lunch on his own, she noticed some cherry stones on a plate. Yielding to temptation, she picked one up and slipped it inside her glove.

Some weeks later the composer returned the other's visit, when she proudly showed him what was now her most treasured piece of jewellery, a brooch on which was mounted the cherry stone encircled with diamonds. 'It bears your teeth marks,' she ended blissfully, after confessing her theft.

Gounod shook his head. 'I never eat cherries,' he explained, 'but my footman always brings them to the table when in season so that he can eat them himself on clearing.'

'*Mon dieu,*' cried the Countess, 'and to think that I almost swallowed one!'

It was not long before another version of this tale began circulating, in which it was the Countess who had been visited by Gounod in the first instance and one of his trouser buttons had been found by her on the carpet after his departure. This she kept and had encased in the finest gold locket she could buy, which she wore on a chain round her neck. Later she called on the composer's wife, who admired the exquisite medallion on the outside of the locket.

'Yes,' agreed the Countess, 'it is beautiful, but it ought to be beautiful to be worthy of what it encloses. Look!' She opened the locket, and Mme Gounod saw to her amazement a trouser button.

'To which great man do you think it belonged?' went on the visitor.

'To the great Napoleon?' her puzzled hostess suggested.

'Oh, no – to someone far greater in my estimation – your husband.'

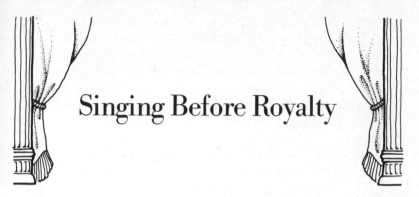

Singing Before Royalty

The admiration many divas have appreciated most has come from royalty. 'Which crowned head do you like best?' Henry Sutherland Edwards, the critic, once asked Patti, who answered: 'The Tsar Alexander gives the best jewellery.' From him she also received his Order of Merit, set in brilliants; was appointed Court Singer; and was permitted to call him 'papa' – whilst the Tsarina, according to Adelina, made tea for her in a samovar between the acts at the St Petersburg opera house.

When Jenny Lind first sang in Vienna, the Dowager Empress, ignoring court convention, threw her own bouquet at the Swedish Nightingale's feet, and later in London Queen Victoria did likewise, in addition giving her a nightingale fashioned entirely out of gems to wear in her hair. The Queen and Prince Albert loved opera. In 1840 they attended twenty-nine performances, and the following year twenty-seven. There was only one work she never patronized and that was *Rigoletto* because she considered its plot immoral.

The son of the Tsar Patti enchanted fell under Melba's spell, presenting her with a magnificent bracelet of engraved diamond cubes and large pearls strung together on a platinum and gold chain, whilst Oscar, King of Norway and Sweden, whom Dame Nellie dubbed her 'smiling giant', rose and bowed to her from his box not once but twice when he first heard her sing at the Royal Opera in Stockholm. Later in Paris, Oscar paid her a surprise visit, revealed he would have much preferred to have been a professional tenor than a king, and saying, 'Imagine I am Jean de Reszke', sang duets with her for almost three hours.

Melba's most gossiped-about success with royalty was her affair with the pretender to the French throne, Louis-Robert-Philippe, Duc d'Orléans, which was built up into a Ruritanian romance by the popular press. Some of her own actions contributed to this, such as when he was exiled from France by its Republican régime and she wagered she could smuggle him into that country from Germany and back, a bet she won by disguising the Duke as her coachman.

There were occasions, on the other hand, when Melba's relations with royals were less happy. Once at La Scala when she was playing the title role in *Lucia di Lammermoor*, her love duet with Edgardo ended abruptly as the orchestra started the Italian national anthem because their Queen had just arrived. Mentioning this in her memoirs, Melba wrote: 'How can I stop in the middle of a tense scene and be expected to continue? One's operatic emotions may be fairly elastic but they are not as elastic as all that.'

It was in 1890, only three years after her début in Brussels, that Melba was first commanded by Queen Victoria to sing at Windsor Castle during a visit of the German Empress. Although the recital was supposed to start at four o'clock, it was half past the hour when she, Jean and Edouard de Reszke, and Francesco Paolo Tosti were shown into the royal presence. After questioning them about their careers, the Queen said as it struck five: 'The Empress is very late returning from her drive. I think we will begin.'

Nellie and the de Reszkes, accompanied by Tosti at the piano, sang for half an hour when the absentee arrived, much to their relief for they were wondering how they could reach Covent Garden in time for the evening performance. But to their dismay the Queen told the Empress: 'What a treat you have missed! We must have more for you.' So the artists were obliged to repeat their programme, doing this in such a hurry that Melba later wrote: 'The trio from *Faust* must have sounded almost like ragtime.'

At ten past six, Nellie managed to explain the position in a whisper to a lady-in-waiting, who told the Queen, and they were allowed to leave – but they finally rushed into the opera house after the curtain had risen, leaving Melba only a few minutes to scramble into costume as Gilda before her cue came. Victoria was unpopular with her after that. When years later someone suggested that she resembled the old Queen, Nellie retorted: 'Don't say that – I hated the bloody woman.'

Also disliked by the diva was Victoria's grandson, Kaiser Wilhelm II, because after a performance of *Lucia di Lammermoor* at the Berlin Opera House he had her summoned to his box where he criticized her rendering of the part. Assuming her most regal manner, Melba thanked him icily for his comments but implied that she thought them in bad taste as 'I would not dream of criticizing your government'. At this, he walked out of the box and left the opera house.

The Kaiser was accustomed to having his own way, which had unfortunate consequences on occasion. For example, in April 1902, Ethel Smyth's one-act music drama *Der Wald* had its première in Berlin with Karl Muck conducting. After the event the *New York Musical Courier* for 14 April carried this report from its German correspondent:

At the final rehearsal, Dr. Muck laid down his baton and uttered the ominous words: *'So geht's nicht!'* His Majesty, Emperor William II, however, insisted upon a production of the work at the Royal Opera House, where his wish, of course, is command. Who, however, is Miss Smyth that she should so prevail upon the Emperor so as to have her opera produced? . . . Her sister is first lady-in-waiting upon the present Queen of England. Be that as it may, Miss Smyth's influence must be a very potent one, and she used it for her own discomfort, for she brought upon her virginal head a fiasco the like of which I have never witnessed.

In 1855 Richard Wagner wrote from London to his wife following a successful concert of his music:

I am quite hoarse with too much talking to – the Queen! . . . Don't think this is a joke. It is all true. The Queen of England has had a long conversation with me. Further I can assure you that she is *not* fat, very short and not at all pretty, with, I am sorry to say, a red nose. Still there is something uncommonly friendly and easy about her and, although she is decidedly not a person of great weight, she is pleasing and amiable. She does not care for instrumental music and when she attends a concert she does it for the sake of her husband who goes in for music and is fond of German instrumental music. But this time she seems to have been impressed. Sainton (the leader of the orchestra) who kept his eye on her all the time, declared that she followed my conducting and the pieces we played with quite unusual and increasing interest; she and Prince Albert were quite stirred by *Tannhäuser* in particular. So much is certain: that when I turned round at the close of the overture both applauded most heartily, smiling at me in a most friendly manner. Naturally the audience backed them up.

During the interval Wagner was presented to the Queen.

I confess I was really touched when this kind and gracious Queen assured me quite simply that she was pleased to make my acquaintance, because I could not help remembering what my ostensible standing with her was – one that could not well be more difficult and embarrassing. Here was I, pursued by the police in Germany like a highway robber, difficulties made about my passport in France, yet received by the Queen of England before the most aristocratic Court in the world with unembarrassed friendliness. That is really quite charming.

Edward VII, like his parents, was genuinely interested in music, particularly that by British composers, and he was also a discerning critic. Once, a celebrated Violetta, instead of dying at Covent Garden in the customary decorous manner, accidentally tumbled off the sofa and landed on the stage in an ungainly heap. The King had the manager, Neil Forsyth, called to his box, and told him: 'It would not be wise for Madame to die in such a dramatic manner again, for she might bruise herself and show too much lingerie.'

The monarch used to have superb eight-course suppers served on gala nights in the anteroom to his box, and insisted that all in the orchestra should be in full evening dress with black ties. 'They ought to look brilliant as they play,' he stressed to Forsyth. On another occasion he noticed that Cleofonte Campanini wore a black tie and was without gloves, so he asked Neil to 'Please gently explain to the *maestro* that it is *de rigueur* at the Royal Opera House for conductors to wear white gloves and white ties. If this is ignored, we shall soon have them smoking cutty pipes and turning the place into a penny gaff.'

When the manager came back to the royal box, he explained that a close relative of Campanini had passed away which was the reason for his black tie. 'I am sorry to hear that,' the King then said, 'but somebody ought to tell him that it is unusual in England for a person in mourning to have on a white waistcoat when wearing evening dress.'

Whilst still Prince of Wales, Edward pointed out to Forsyth how helpful it would be to patrons of Covent Garden with many social functions to attend if the times acts began and ended were printed in the programme. 'I should then know when to get to the Opera for a particular scene if, through other engagements, I am unable to sit through the work.' As a result, every afternoon a programme with these details for that evening's performance was sent to Marlborough House when the Prince was in town. Once it was suggested that the entr'actes might be cut so that he could attend a ball at eleven, but he refused, saying: 'Don't hurry the artists. If you hustle them, they won't sing at their best, and I should not like the audience to be disappointed.'

Like his mother, Edward VII held concerts at Windsor Castle in honour of visiting royalty. On one occasion things went wrong from start to finish. This was in November 1905, when he asked his guest and brother-in-law, the King of the Hellenes, if there were any singer he would particularly like to hear; he chose Mary Garden, who had just made a successful début in London. This created an embarrassing situation, for Edward had already commanded Melba's services and it was then the custom to invite only one soprano, one tenor and so on, in order to avoid any rivalry among the artists.

It was not until the two proud divas arrived in the Grand Saloon on the evening of the concert that they discovered, to their great annoyance, that both were included in the programme. Sir Lionel Cust has recorded how, when the pair took their places beside each other on the sofa reserved for them in full view of the audience, they could not conceal their mutual dislike, which roused much amusement.

At the request of the tenor Zenatello, a second piano lowered a tone or so had been provided to suit his voice, but Landon Ronald forgot about this and started to accompany him on the instrument he had just used for Miss Garden. Zenatello faltered and almost lost his head, but recovered enough somehow or other to get through his aria from Boito's *Mefistofele*.

There was further trouble. Determined to satisfy his own preference for classical music, the Master of the King's Musick, Sir Walter Parratt, had arranged for the Hungarian violinist, Veczey, to take part, and had advised the young prodigy to play Bach's *Chaconne*. The royal party after a day's shooting and a banquet were not in the mood for listening to a long, unaccompanied violin solo. Sir Lionel could see King Edward becoming increasingly restless and considered it an error of judgement for Parratt to have inserted the *Chaconne* between Melba 'in the familiar *"Caro nome"* ' and Zenatello 'in an already hackneyed song from *Pagliacci*'. Cust comments: 'It was a relief to be out in St George's Hall for supper.'

But Mary Garden found the meal itself a trial. In her reminiscences, she relates how Melba, who was only two chairs away from her, remarked loudly: 'What a dreadful concert this would have been if I hadn't come!' Very embarrassed, Lord Farquhar began to pay Mary a compliment to cover up the other's insult, but the Scottish-born soprano raised her hand and said: 'Please don't bother about me. I love Melba's rudeness. It amuses me.'

When asked if they would care to spend the night in the Castle or be taken back to London in the private train, both women decided to do the latter, for they had sung in an extremely chilly room. Mary, in fact, caught a severe cold and spent three weeks in bed at the Savoy with, according to her, 'the most wretched laryngitis and tonsilitis'. She also says that before they reached the capital, Melba and she were fast friends. 'During the journey she turned to me and said: "Mary, I want you to tell me how to act Tosca. I've been studying it, and there are a lot of things about it that puzzle me. What sort of a wig should I wear?" '

Mary Garden told her companion all she could about the role, but secretly regarded it as a waste of time as the other was in every way unsuited to singing Tosca, and in fact never did. Their friendship, however, lasted because the fact that Mary was not a coloratura like Melba prevented her from being a serious rival, and because they both loved gambling together at Monte Carlo. So after all there was for these two a happy ending to their royal command concert.

Edward VII's second brother, Alfred, Duke of Edinburgh, was

an excellent violinist who played *obbligatos* for Christine Nilsson, Minnie Hauk and Emma Albani at public concerts, whilst the King's eldest daughter, the Duchess of Fife, was a music-lover with a highly sensitive ear. When she attended a performance of *Fidelio* at Drury Lane, the Duchess brought with her two huge orchestral scores, then sat on the floor of her box reading one of them intently and turning over the leaves during the *stretto* of the *Leonora* overture. Suddenly she noticed an uncertain note from the second horn and exclaimed as if to set the musician right: 'B flat!' Later, the conductor, Sir Michael Costa, was asked whether something did not go wrong with one of the horns. 'Yes,' he replied, 'but only a person with a very fine ear could have noticed it.'

Leopold II, King of the Belgians, a cousin of both Queen Victoria and Prince Albert, had no ear whatever for music. He could not make out a melody, and it is said that one day when listening attentively to the playing of the *Brabaçonne*, his national anthem, he turned round to his secretary and declared proudly: 'Well, this time I have got it – this is the *Marseillaise*.' On another occasion, hearing the *Marseillaise*, he exclaimed: 'Now I am sure I am right – this is the *Brabaçonne!*'

Monarchs who do not appreciate opera's charms find that attending performances is an ordeal. George V told Sir Thomas Beecham that *La Bohème* was his favourite such work, but only because it was the shortest. Ivor Newton relates in *At the Piano* how when the King attended a gala concert at the Albert Hall the singers were all accompanied by the orchestra, but Conchita Supervia, who appeared late in the programme, insisted on singing with piano accompaniment. 'For some reason, perhaps the intimacy that contrasts so strongly with orchestral music, songs with piano accompaniment invariably arouse great enthusiasm at an orchestral concert – a fact that Supervia must have known perfectly well – and her songs this evening were no exception to the rule; she was wearing a wonderful flamenco dress the train of which swept hugely behind her.' Two encores were demanded by the audience, and as Newton was standing in the artists' room expecting a third, Sir Walford Davies, the Master of the King's Musick, who was in attendance on the King and had run all the way from the royal box, rushed breathlessly up to Ivor and told

him: 'The King is very angry. His Majesty thought it was to be
understood that there are to be no encores while he is present. He
says that nothing will keep him in the Hall a moment after half-past
ten.'

The time was then twenty-past ten. Richard Tauber had yet to
sing, and the concert was due to end with the Hungarian March
from Berlioz's *Damnation of Faust*. Newton appealed to Sir
Henry Wood who was to conduct the rest of the programme. He
hustled Tauber on to the stage before the applause for Supervia
had ceased, hurried him through his aria, waved him off again
despite his indignation after a single bow and swept the orchestra
into Berlioz's *March*, which must never before have been played
so fast. And so, thanks to Wood's efficiency and his stop-watch
mind, the concert finished on the stroke of ten-thirty and disaster
was averted.

Ernest Newman, when musical critic of *The Birmingham Post*,
reviewed in its columns in 1911 Emma Albani's memoirs, *Forty
Years of Song*. He commented that the crowning joy of all for a
prima donna was when monarchs wrote their names 'with their
very hands in her autograph book'. In Mme Albani's 'dazzling'
chapter with the 'golden' title, 'Singing Before Royalty', she
revealed that even greater monarchs than those of Europe had not
disdained to show her honour.

Did not that acute critic of singing, King Kalakua of the Sandwich Islands,
compliment her, and was she not, as might be expected 'very gratified by
his kindness', and did he not decorate her with the Sandwich Islands
Order of Merit? There can have been nothing quite equal in pathos to this
touching scene since the historic day when Tartarin of Tarascon and the
African King rubbed noses together and swore eternal fidelity to each
other. The heart of the bored reviewer goes out to his Serene Majesty King
Kalakua and to the Chinese Ambassador who went to sleep and snored
audibly to the scandal of everyone, at a concert at Buckingham Palace;
they seem the only real, natural human beings in all these mellifluous
saccharine pages.

Canadian-born Emma Albani, whose real name was Marie de
Lajeunesse, sang regularly at Covent Garden from 1872 to 1896,
and married its director, Ernest Gye, son of the impresario

Frederick Gye, who managed the opera house from 1849 to 1877 with such devotion and who has a more permanent memorial than the compliments of monarchs, for his statue still stands there today – near the entrance to the gentlemen's cloakroom.

'Your Majesty, this is the Royal Command Performance.
You plant the tree tomorrow!'

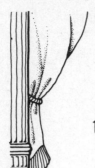
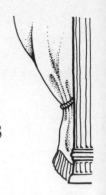

Audiences in
the 'Good' Old Days

Unfortunately for the ageing Queen of Song there are few reigning monarchs left to grace the boxes at her farewells. She longs for the good old days – but were the old days always so good? Many opera-goers have suffered from the noise caused by others during the performance, but it was far worse in the past. For example, in Venice in the early eighteenth century patricians came masked to the opera so that they might enjoy a *tête-à-tête* or a tumble with their mistresses in the curtained privacy of their boxes. They roistered with no regard for what was taking place on the stage. Those above the pit would amuse themselves by throwing down lighted spills, and the sight of a bald head led to a spitting contest. Young blades on their own ogled outrageously all the girls singing in the chorus or dancing in the ballet. The leading male singers, overdressed in finery whatever their role, would strut about the stage taking snuff, chatting with the prompter and openly flirting with any of the fair sex in the audience who took their fancy. As for the virtuosas, their main concern was to catch the laudatory verses rained down on them and to smile at those who shouted compliments.

Armand von Uffench, Mayor of Frankfurt, visited Venice for the Carnival in 1714 and attended a performance at the largest opera house, the San Giovanni e Paolo. He wrote that he was astonished when the aristocrats sitting in their boxes started to spit tobacco as well as apple and orange peel down below, aiming in particular at the women wearing the most attractive masks. He was hit several times, which annoyed him as he was bareheaded, and wished he could have revenged himself. The only solution was to rent a box and behave in the same way.

Benedetto Marcello, satirizing manners in Venice at that time, wrote that those in high society should know nothing about music, staging or ballet. 'They will buy their tickets on approval and leave every night after fifteen minutes.' This was so that they could be refunded the admission charge. 'Thus they see the entire opera in twelve evenings.'

If the opera should fail to attract the paying public, then, Marcello continues, 'Every night the impresario will hand out complimentary tickets to his doctor, lawyer, pharmacist, banker, carpenter, and their business partners, also to his friends with their families.' Should this fail to fill the auditorium, the gondoliers must be urged to take advantage of their recognized right to free seats (though not to boxes empty on account of a death in the family).

Opera in those days can best be described as concerts in costume that followed a fixed succession of hackneyed situations, with the action being so contrived that each principal was allotted the number of arias proper to his or her place in the vocal hierarchy. Movement on the stage was minimal, with the principals taking up positions – centre, right or left – according to the same code of operatic precedence.

Dr Charles Burney in *The Present State of Music in France and Italy* gave his impressions of the old Scala in Milan when he attended an opera there in 1770.

The theatre here is very splendid; it has five rows of boxes on each side, one hundred in each row and parallel to these runs a broad gallery round the house, as an avenue to every row of boxes: each box will contain six persons, who sit at the sides, facing each other. Across the gallery of communication is a complete room to every box with a fireplace in it, and all conveniences for refreshments and cards. In the fourth row is a faro table on each side of the house, which is used during the performance of the opera.

As a result, 'the noise was abominable, except while two or three airs and a duet were being sung with which everyone was in raptures'.

Boswell, describing a visit to the Scala five years earlier, wrote: 'Rough dogs often roared out "Brava". The singers seemed slovenly. Blackguard boys held the sweeping female trains and often let them go to scratch their head or blow their nose with their finger. I wished to have had gingerbread or liquorice to give them.'

On 3 August 1778 the new Scala was opened. Spacious, comfortable, adequately heated, it was the most attractive communal centre in Milan, and so that its revenues might be sufficient to maintain it, gambling was allowed by the authorities, and at the tables ladies were to be found most of the evening, for once they had heard an opera they only occupied their seats in the auditorium when they felt like listening to their favourite arias. And to learn the latest scandals in confidence and then to discuss and pass them on, they would circulate in the corridors and anterooms. As for the men, it was politics, business matters and love affairs that they discussed in the auditorium, mostly oblivious of what was happening on the stage.

It was soon found that there was insufficient support for the works of Cimarosa, Paisiello and Zingarelli for the Scala's programmes to be entirely operatic. In fact, during the first ten years only twenty-two different operas were produced, and on occasion La Scala almost became a circus when its stage was occupied by acrobats, jugglers, tightrope-walkers, puppet shows and the like.

Thirty-six years after Charles Burney recorded this, Stendhal wrote, after his own travels: 'In Italy, a lady's box is a salon . . . where her friends present themselves as soon as they see her arrive with her lover.' Regarding La Scala, he said: 'The public is silent only on first nights and on later nights only when one comes to the *beaux morceaux*. People who want to listen to the whole opera seek out places in the parterre, which is immense, furnished with excellent benches with backs, where one is quite comfortable, so comfortable in fact that English visitors indignantly count twenty or thirty sleepers.'

Describing a visit to the San Carlo, Stendhal wrote: 'Nothing can give the remotest idea of the rage of a Neapolitan audience on being insulted by a wrong note.' He found the audience attending the world première of Rossini's *La donna del lago* hostile from the rise of the curtain, clearly awaiting a chance to riot. This occurred when Nozzari the tenor sang flat in the prolonged *portamento* on his first entrance. The effect was as if 'a cage of roaring, ravenous lions had been let loose' or as if 'Aeolus had unleashed the fury of the winds!'

Despite this, the cast soldiered on to the end. At one juncture, five rows of drunks stood in front of the orchestra and accompanied the trumpet passages by banging their walking sticks on chairs and the floor, imitating the galloping of horses, and the rest of the audience soon joined in the fracas.

This was too much for Rossini. He fled and took refuge in Colbran's dressing-room, where one of the management staff found him after the opera had somehow finished and pressed him to take a curtain call. For answer, the exasperated composer knocked the man out with a right to the jaw.

In his reminiscences, published in 1826, the composer Michael Kelly gives an amusing account of how seriously the inhabitants of Rome took visits to the opera. The numerous abbés were the severest critics. They would sit in the front row of the pit, each holding in one hand a lighted taper and in the other the score of the opera, and should an unfortunate singer make a mistake, they would cry out: *'Bravo, bestia!'* The composer would preside at the piano during the first three performances of his work, and should any passage strike the audience as similar to the melody of another composer, the theft would be denounced with shouts of *'Bravo, il ladro!'* or *'Bravo, Paisiello!'* or *'Bravo, Sacchini!'* if they considered these composers had been plagiarized.

Cimarosa once at the Teatro della Valle used a movement in an opera which reminded the audience of a theme from another of his works which he had written for the previous Carnival Season. An abbé noticed this at once and, jumping to his feet, thundered: *'Bravo, Cimarosa! Welcome back from Naples. By your music tonight, it is clear that you have brought a trunk full of stale food with you. You are an excellent cook for hashing up old dishes!'*

A few years later Mendelssohn had this to say about a visit to a Roman première: 'When Pacini's grand finale began, the whole pit stood up, talking to each other as loudly as they could, laughing and turning their backs to the stage. Mme Samoilow fainted in her box and was carried out. Pacini stole away from the piano, and at the end of the act the curtain fell in the midst of great tumult.'

At Covent Garden, too, there has been trouble at various times. In February 1763, when the prices were increased for Arne's successful opera *Artaxerxes*, a riot resulted. The report in the *Gentleman's Magazine* for 23 February read:

The mischief done was the greatest ever known on any occasion of the like kind; all the benches of the boxes and pit being entirely torn up, the glasses and chandeliers broken, and the linings of the boxes cut to pieces. The rashness of the rioters was so great that they cut away the wooden pillars between the boxes, so that if the inside of them had not been iron, they would have brought the galleries down upon their heads. The damages done amount to at least £2000. Four persons concern'd in the riot have been committed to the Gatehouse.

There were no further riots, but cat-calls and hissing disturbed performances to such an extent that John Beard, the opera house's proprietor and manager, eventually reduced the prices for *Artaxerxes*.

Audiences then stayed relatively peaceful at Covent Garden until 1801, when a drunk in the gallery flung a gin bottle at a singer on the stage, causing such pandemonium that five guardsmen with fixed bayonets were needed to restore order in the gallery. Seven years later the theatre was burned down, and in order to recoup some of the cost of rebuilding, prices were raised by Kemble. Resentment at this, inflamed by the news of the enormous fees he had agreed to pay Catalani, was the cause of the notorious 'OP' riots.

Kemble was foolish enough to select *Macbeth* with which to reopen on 18 September 1809, and it certainly brought bad luck. Shouts of 'Old prices!' rang out from all over the auditorium throughout the evening, and when the actor-manager attempted to plead for quiet, Covent Garden turned into a veritable bear-garden, and the police, reinforced by the military, were hastily summoned and the Riot Act read.

Defiantly, Kemble refused at first to reduce prices, but after sixty-one nights of noisy protests by audiences wearing 'OP' badges on hats and coats and waving 'OP' banners, he was forced to give way.

One might have expected better behaviour where 'polite' society came as guests to a noble lord's mansion for the purpose of listening to superb operatic singing, especially when they could enjoy the added attraction of a celebrated composer playing his own music at the piano.

After such an event, Weber wrote to his wife from London on 12 March 1826:

Audiences in the 'Good' Old Days

At half-past ten I drove to Lord Hertford's. Heavens, what a vast assembly! A magnificent room, 500–600 people there, all of the greatest brilliance. Almost the entire Italian opera company. . . . Some *finales* were sung, etc., but not a soul listened. The shrieking and jabbering of this throng of humanity was atrocious. While I played, they tried to get a little quiet and circa 100 people gathered round, displaying the greatest interest. But what they can have heard, God alone knows, for I myself heard very little of it. Meanwhile I thought hard about my 30 guineas, and so was perfectly patient.

Another composer, Puccini, on a visit to London in 1900, was invited by Melba's patroness, Lady de Grey, to share her box at Covent Garden. Afterwards he told a friend that it had proved impossible to concentrate his attention on the stage because of the almost continuous chatter of his hostess and her other guests. The experience made him now believe the tale he had heard of a garrulous English dowager who had given up her box on losing her voice.

Recording for Posterity

Memoirs, diaries and letters are the most reliable sources to explore when seeking to discover what the past was really like. As far as the human voice is concerned, since the commencement of this century we have been able to judge for ourselves through the gramophone. Singers are thus assured of some measure of immortality. Recording in the early days was an ordeal.

Eldridge Johnson, founder of Victor Talking Machines, said that singers often sounded like 'a partially educated parrot with a sore throat and a cold in the head'. Even by the start of the 1920s conditions in the studios themselves had hardly improved. Sir Malcolm Sargent once vividly recollected his experiences thus: 'We were so cramped that I had to stand on a shelf, strapped to the wall so that I couldn't fall off. While conducting with my right hand I kept my left hand on the soprano's head, pushing her towards the horn on low notes to "bump" them up and pulling her back from it on high ones to avoid "blast". For one of his entries, the baritone had to crawl under the violinists' elbows, surface just in front of the horn, bob down and crawl back. We must have looked as funny as any Marx Brothers' film. The results sounded remarkably good for all that.'

Some eighteen years previously, the head office of the Gramophone Company in Maiden Lane, London, had failed to impress its visitors. After careful coaxing, Fred Gaisberg persuaded Emma Calvé to go there and make recordings, but no sooner had Landon Ronald helped her out of the elegant four-wheeler outside the narrow entrance to the derelict-looking building than, staring with horror at it, she cried: '*Mon dieu, quel trou!* Never will I enter such a place. It is a tavern – not a manufactory! I shall be robbed

136

there – I feel it in my bones! You have brought me to a thieves' den!'

Ronald pleaded that everything had been prepared, but she climbed back into the vehicle and nothing would make her leave it. The other, experienced in dealing with difficult divas, had an idea and running upstairs into the office told Gaisberg what had happened and made a suggestion for solving the problem. Shortly afterwards, Ronald returned to Calvé who was in a fury at having been left alone, but her anger was snuffed out when from a bag he poured on to her lap one hundred and ten gold sovereigns – the sum agreed for six recordings, now paid in advance. In a trice, she had gathered them up. '*Allons, mon petit* Ronald!' Calvé cried, throwing on her mantilla, and out of the four-wheeler she leapt.

Progress in the studio, however, was slow, for recordings were constantly being spoilt by Emma's shrieks of delight or dissatisfaction after singing a phrase, according to how she regarded her rendering; and when they reached the Seguidilla from *Carmen*, nothing could dissuade her from dancing as on the stage in front of the horn.

Gerald Moore, in *Am I Too Loud?*, has given a fascinating account of recording for HMV in Hayes, Middlesex in 1921. The studio walls were of unpolished deal and the floor of hardwood, and in the absence of sound-absorbent material his footsteps thundered on the bare boards and his voice boomed as if his head were 'in the resounding womb of some giant double-bass'. A huge horn protruded into the room connecting it with the machine chamber, gathering sound and recording it on the soft wax disc. The singer would have his or her head half-way down the horn. 'Only the piano could be moved, now here, now there, and I would frequently find myself, by the time the balance was adjusted and we were ready to make the master recording, with a bird's-eye view of the singer; his buttocks were all I could see of him, while my piano would be as far away as the length of a billiards-room. It is vital for the accompanist to hear what the singer is doing and my difficulties under these conditions can be imagined since his sounds were not emanating from the end of him nearest to me.'

The recording of duets, Moore reveals, often developed into 'a free-for-all . . . each wanted to hog the trumpet'. He marvelled that they had any breath left for singing. Arthur Clark, then head recording engineer, would give them one buzz to prepare, two buzzes for silence, and finally a red light to tell them to begin. 'Runners in a hundred-yard sprint were not quicker off the mark than we. This, in fact, is how Selma Kurz – that wonderful soprano from the Vienna State Opera – and I endeavoured to record Beethoven's 'Adelaide', a lengthy song with an extremely slow first section. Long before we had finished this *larghetto* we were buzzed by the engineer, who put his head through the window to inform us that he had come to the end of the wax. We tried again and now I played my introduction at a speed that would have shocked Beethoven, but Mme. Kurz was standing so far from the piano, with her head in the trumpet, that not hearing me, and no blame to her, she became slower and slower. I am afraid we had to abandon poor Adelaide.'

Already, at the age of twenty-two, Gerald Moore had become experienced as a recording artist, but he says that any complacency he might have felt was rudely shattered by the arrival of Melba on the scene. 'I should probably have lost my life at her hands, had not the diminutive Fred Gaisberg, recording manager, been in control.' She came to the studio, some time after her retirement, with a protégée, Elena Danieli, to listen to her recording.

Deciding that young Moore was inexperienced and easily frightened, Melba enjoyed herself by bullying him. 'Can't you find somebody,' she shrieked at last, 'who can get a good tune out of the piano?' She glared at him. 'He plays so hard.'

'Listen, Dame Nellie,' retorted Fred, who could be a lion-tamer. 'You just leave this boy alone. Come and sit in the recording-room with me and you will find that he and Miss Danieli will make good records.'

Gerald Moore goes on: 'The great woman looked him up and down – a process that did not take much time with Gaisberg – but Fred turned on his heel and sauntered out of the studio. She followed like a lamb.'

Fred Gaisberg had, of course, known Melba long. It was he who in 1904 first persuaded her to record for the Gramophone Company and she insisted on this being done in her own drawing-room, when he says he found her 'a dominant, harsh Queen who made no attempt to clothe her speech with honeyed words' and who was 'caustic enough about the process' but sufficiently interested to keep everyone busy through a long day. There was much hard bargaining before she signed a contract that granted all her demands. A mauve label bearing a reproduction of her autograph was to be fixed to every record and she was to be paid a royalty of 23 per cent on the selling price, which was not to be less than one guinea as Caruso's were priced at a sovereign. The experiment proved an outstanding success. The public rushed to buy the first pressings, which were all sold within a few days.

As Maggie Teyte once pointed out: 'When we talk or sing, we become deaf.' Before recording was invented, the only way a singer could discover how his voice really sounded was by holding his palms over his ears, a method Mario del Monaco adopted at rehearsals. As he could hardly do that when performing on the stage, he would fix nose putty behind his ears so as to cover the orifice with the flaps.

When Laurence Tibbett learnt of this from Robert Merrill, he tried it out, but packed so much putty behind both ears that the audience laughed for it looked as if he were wearing headphones on a spaceship.

Caruso was his own severest critic and he was particularly sensitive about the artistic value of his records, believing that only half a dozen gave a true reproduction of his voice. One evening in his New York apartment he played some, telling his guests they were his latest which had not yet been released. After listening to a superb tenor voice singing Italian folk songs, all present applauded spontaneously and told him they were his finest discs to date. No one living or dead could have approached such singing was the unanimous verdict.

'No more – please!' Caruso interrupted. 'It makes me too sad. These are not mine at all. They were made by an unknown tenor who is not even included in the catalogue of the better artists.'

With live performances, too, Caruso suspected that a great deal of a singer's reputation depended upon uncritical adulation and clever publicity rather than intrinsic merit. He often set traps for the unwary to confirm such a belief. One evening at the Metropolitan Albert Reiss, a tenor of the second rank, was in his dressing-room when hardly had the curtain risen on *I pagliacci* than Caruso came in to ask a favour. Could he, Caruso, sing the serenade that Reiss in his role sang off-stage? Though mystified by the request, Albert agreed. After Caruso had sung the aria in this fashion, there was no applause, neither did any critic next day in the newspapers comment, as might have been expected, that Reiss had surpassed himself when singing the serenade.

'You see, it is not Caruso they want,' Enrico told the other, 'it is only the knowledge that they are hearing Caruso.'

The record producer George Martin relates in *All You Need Is Ears* how, when he was with EMI, Kirsten Flagstad was unwell when making a recording and could not sing her top C. It was impossible for her to return another day and as the rest of her performance was magnificent, Elisabeth Schwarzkopf, who was in the building, agreed to dub in the high C. Those involved promised to keep the matter a secret, but someone was indiscreet and revealed all to the press. It caused quite a stir, but Martin comments that he could not understand why such a fuss was made: 'Everyone has his off days, and if you're going to make a great record, why not dub in the one note? After all, it wasn't as if it was something the main singer couldn't do at all. On any other day she could have done it perfectly well.'

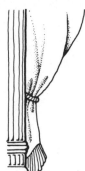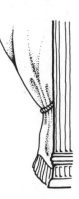

What They Thought Back Home

Our diva can rise no higher. She has recorded for posterity, kings have fêted her, and she owns her own weight in jewels. Now at long last she returns to the obscure place where she was born. It is the greatest day in its history.

Emma Calvé tells in her autobiography how when famous she went back to her native village, where the Mayor rang the tocsin, summoned the peasants from their work in the fields and had them all gathered together before the town hall. Then he addressed them: 'I have brought you here to listen to a little nightingale of these parts. It will sing to you from this very window. Listen well and I am sure you will acclaim our accomplished compatriot, Mlle Emma.'

Calvé sang to them a selection of the arias that had won her international acclaim, but they listened in complete silence. Amazed and distressed, she went down and approached an old shepherd friend. 'Blaise, what's the matter?' she asked. 'Why didn't you clap or cheer? Did I sing as badly as all that?'

The old man could scarcely conceal his emotion. 'Poor child, poor girl,' he quavered. 'How you scream! How it must hurt you! You are wearing out your life! You are wearing it out! Such a waste of strength. It's dreadful!'

A similar reaction came from some Indian braves visiting New York who had never heard an operatic singer before and whom Barnum invited to hear Jenny Lind. Afterwards, asked for their opinion, one replied: 'She made a very big noise then a little noise. The white man must have a great deal more money than he needs to hear this lady sing.'

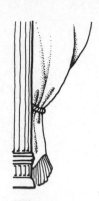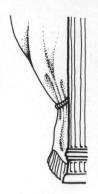

The Opera that
Shocked America

When a singer has reached the summit and is still comparatively young, she may wonder what next to attempt. Something provocative? Why not? Years ago, outrageously daring, she might have chosen *Salomé*. Strange as it may seem today it is the only opera that has really shocked America. No opera by Richard Strauss had been presented there till then, and its première, in January 1907, might have proved an uncontroversial event if Heinrich Conried, then managing the Metropolitan, had not decided on *Salomé*. He was also unwise enough to hold the dress rehearsal on a Sunday and to throw the opera house open to over a thousand people, a great number of whom had come straight from church. As might have been anticipated, the sight of Olive Fremstad caressing John the Baptist's severed head upset them considerably more than might have been the case had Conried held the preview on a weekday.

At the actual première, a stream of prominent opera-goers hurried out and the next day it became the major sensation of all the newspapers. One report began: 'Many voices were hushed as the crowd passed out into the night, many faces were white . . . many women were silent and men spoke as if a bad dream were upon them.' The redoubtable critic Henry E. Krehbiel wrote in the *New York Tribune* for 23 January that his conscience was 'stung into righteous fury by the moral stench with which *Salomé* fills the nostrils of mankind'. The music offended the ear and rasped the nerves 'like fiddlestrings played on by a coarse file'. There was not a 'whiff of fresh and healthy air blowing through *Salomé* except that which exudes from the cistern'. He ended: 'The orchestra

shrieked its final horror and left the listeners staring at each other
with smarting eyeballs and wrecked nerves.'

Richard Aldrich in the *New York Times* attacked the theme as
'abhorrent'. The other leading critic, W J Henderson, of the *Sun*,
thought that Miss Fremstad 'coddled' the head a good deal more at
the dress rehearsal than on the first night 'when she moderated her
transports so that even little girls . . . were not shocked'. As for the
society women, they viewed the spectacle with perfect calmness'.
He commented at length on the score:

Strauss has a mania for writing ugly music: a modern harpy, he cannot
touch anything without besmearing it with dissonance. What more natural
than that he should cast about for a subject which imperatively demands
hideous din to correspond with and justify his concatenated discords? And
what more natural than that the noisome Salomé should seem an ideal
companion for his noisy music? The presentation of such a story is a
crime. Richard Strauss' music is aesthetically criminal or at least
extremely coarse and ill-mannered. His music often suggests a man who
comes to a social reception unkempt, with hands unwashed, cigar in
mouth, hat on, and who sits down and puts his feet on the table. No boor
ever violated all the laws of etiquette as Strauss violates all the laws of
musical composition. There is one consolation. Thanks to the prevailing
dissonance, nobody knows or cares whether the singers sing the right notes
– that is, the notes assigned to them – or not. Who can fail to see the
stupendous originality of Richard Strauss? What composer before him has
been so clever as to be able to write music in which it makes no difference
whether or not you sing or play correctly?

Letters from the public, mostly hostile, appeared in the press.
One from a physician in the *New York Times* for 24 January read:
'I am a man of middle age who has devoted upwards of twenty
years to the practice of a profession that necessitates a daily
intimacy with degeneracy.' What he had seen on the stage of the
Metropolitan was 'one of the most horrible, disgusting, revolting
and unmentionable' exhibitions of degeneracy he had 'ever heard,
read or imagined'. On the other hand an elderly lady wrote that she
had already seen *Salomé* twenty-seven times in Europe and it had
in no way corrupted her morals.

People were still easily shocked in the first decade of this
century. They were scandalized by the sight of Isadora Duncan

dancing with her feet and legs bare, and Chaliapin caused a sensation when he sang the title role in Boito's *Mefistofele* bare-chested.

The exodus from the auditorium on the first night of *Salomé* had been led by Mrs Herbert Satterlee, J. Pierpont Morgan's daughter; that family, together with the Astors and the Vanderbilts, formed the syndicate that, backed by Wall Street finance, kept the Met alive. As a result the Board of the Metropolitan Opera and Real Estate Company passed a resolution that *Salomé* was 'objectionable and detrimental to the best interests of the opera-house' and Conried was told on 27 January to remove it from the repertory. After some resistance he gave way, and on 3 February in the *Sun* W.J. Henderson declared that the cancellation of further performances of this 'operatic offal' had removed 'a stench from the nostrils'. He added: 'If this be art, then let the music of the future find her mission in sewer, pesthouse and brothel.'

Mary Garden relates in her memoirs how towards the end of her first season at Oscar Hammerstein's new Manhattan Opera House, he called her into his office to say that he intended to put on *Salomé*. In view of the trouble its production had caused at the Met the previous year, she suggested that it might prove risky, but he replied that this did not worry him and that he wanted her to play the title role. She agreed on condition that she performed the Dance of the Seven Veils herself – the ballerina, Bianca Froelich, had undertaken this for Olive Fremstad. Mary then went to Paris to be coached by the head teacher of dancing at the *Opéra*. 'I want the Dance to be *drama* – not *Folies Bergères!*' she stressed.

For the Manhattan première, Mary wore very pale pink veils of the thinnest muslin. 'It was an enchanting dance, lovely and classical in feeling,' she claims. 'Everything was glorious and nude and suggestive, but not coarse. Herod wasn't looking for anything coarse in Salomé's dance; he was looking for beauty. I saw them dance the hoochi-koochi once in Algiers, stomachs all bare and rolling. My stomach wasn't bare in *Salomé* and I never rolled it.'

Salomé stirred her more than any other part. It made her feel sensually replete when her lips at last pressed against Jokanaan's mouth. She played the role as a short-haired girl of fifteen 'born in vice and with a poet's face'. This she believed made the subject less likely to offend. The sight of a fully developed woman with bulging breasts and hefty hips indulging her lust would repel. She was proved right, for there were no protests at the first night or after and the production proved enormously successful. Nevertheless, Hammerstein would sit in the wings on the prompt side, cigar in mouth, during every performance waiting for Mary to finish her business with the head in case there was trouble. Then he would straighten his shoulders and go home to bed.

Whilst the critics lauded Garden's characterization, they still disapproved of the opera. Reginald de Koven's comments in the *World* are typical of the general consensus of opinion: 'A sewer is certainly a necessity of our everyday life, but the fact of its existence does not also create the necessity for us to bend over its reeking filth to inhale its mephitic vapors.' After reading such reviews, it is not surprising that the President of the Law and Order League should have written: 'I am a normal man, but I would not trust myself to see a performance of *Salomé*.' Mary Garden countered this with: 'Anyone whose morals could have been corrupted by seeing *Salomé* must already have degenerated.'

A fortnight after the New York opening, Oscar Hammerstein brought the production to his opera house in Philadelphia, despite the protests of the local clergy. According to the *Public Ledger* for the following day, 11 February, over a thousand people queueing for standing room failed to gain admittance, and when the curtain rose twenty minutes late all available space was filled except four boxes, leased by patrons objecting to the opera. Contrary to expectations 'no one left at crucial moments, no women fainted nor men cried hoarsely "Enough, enough!" as the head of the Baptist was handed up from the cistern's depths, as might have been expected, judging from what many have said and written of late.' In fact at the end there was tremendous applause and fourteen curtain calls. Some of the critics praised the music, but all disliked the libretto. William R. Lester in *The North American* thought its 'inspiration might have proceeded from the dread seventh circle of Dante's Inferno'.

Salomé was presented for three performances in Philadelphia, but though audiences were large 'dissension among the established clientèle' grew, reported the *Public Ledger*, and nine boxes in the Grand Tier were left empty. So Hammerstein removed the opera from the repertory and the *New York Sun* quoted him as saying:

People often want to be informed about certain matters that perhaps they think they ought not to know about. Under these circumstances it makes a very bad impression to be the informer. So although I might have continued to have large houses with *Salomé* in Philadelphia, I preferred not to take the risk of being the man that taught Philadelphia anything it thinks it ought not to know.

On 29 March Hammerstein's company opened for a short season in Boston. He had planned to present *Salomé* there, but there was furious opposition and the Mayor wired the impresario: 'If you perform *Salomé* here, we promise to put every one of you in jail.' When Oscar received this, he told Mary Garden that he had a good mind to ignore the threat – 'just for the pleasure of seeing you behind bars'.

It was not until 1922, when Mary was with the Chicago Grand Opera Company, sponsored by the McCormicks, that she was to appear again in America in the controversial role. Every seat for the four performances announced was sold well in advance, and she claims in her memoirs that all went smoothly with no attempts at interference. Vincent Sheean, in *Opera News* for 3 December 1960, wrote that he remembered how she made 'something extraordinarily obsessive out of this juvenile delinquent'. Though she was no longer equal to all the singing, he had never forgotten her performance: 'Nothing like it has been seen since.' Surprisingly, the most vehement adverse comment came from an ill-qualified champion of morality, the notorious Al Capone, who told a *Tribune* reporter after a visit to the opera: 'It was indecent, disgusting – Miss Garden wallowed around like a cat in a bed of cat-mint.' Her retort to this was that indecency, like beauty, was in the eye of the beholder.

The fourth performance of *Salomé* was, however, cancelled – but not on account of the gangster's objections. The decision was conveyed to Mary by Mrs Harold McCormick. 'My dear, I've given three performances – you've occupied your box for each one of them – why can't I give the fourth?' demanded the diva.

'It's you. The truth came to me in a flash when I went home after your third performance,' replied the other.

'And what do you mean by the truth?'

'I said to myself, "Edith, your vibrations are all wrong." '

According to Mary Garden's account, nothing would make the sponsor's wife change her mind, but when the cancellation was made public, an invitation came from Milwaukee for the fourth performance to be given there, which took place successfully in front of an audience of some ten thousand people.

Later in Mary Garden's career, she was to appear in the controversial role at Dallas. As hardly anyone in Texas had heard of *Salomé*, the opera house management engaged a New York publicity expert to persuade people to buy tickets. With those likely to support a show having scriptural associations and a moral message, he expanded on the biblical origin of the plot, describing it as a sort of musical passion play. They were to discover to their discomfiture that it dealt with quite a different sort of passion. With more philistine potential customers, such as tired businessmen, his sales talk gave the impression that the opera was one long strip-tease. As a result of thus appealing to all tastes, every seat was sold for the opening. Soon the audience became restive, some were shocked, most were bored, all were angry – even the Dance of the Seven Veils failed to excite, for Mary Garden was visibly ageing. By the final curtain few remained in the opera house.

It was not till some sixteen years after its New York première that *Salomé* was again presented at the Metropolitan. This was on 13 January 1933, with Ljungberg in the title role. On this occasion Henderson completely reversed his previous judgements and found the 'splendor' of much of the score 'not matched by anything else written since Wagner' and the conductor, Bodanzky, one who made it all sound 'more glorious' than it ever had. The *éclat* was mostly his, for Ljungberg sang stridently and her dance was almost absurd, as when she shed the last of the veils she had on as much as before, and also so as not to offend anybody she fondled the head, a bewigged grapefruit, in the shelter of the prompter's box.

In England, *Salomé* could not be staged without the Lord Chamberlain's permission and that caused Sir Thomas Beecham considerable trouble. In *A Mingled Chime*, he wrote that after the startling success of *Elektra* in 1910 during his first Covent Garden season, it was inevitable that his search for an equal sensation should lead him to *Salomé*, and he engaged for the part slim and beautiful Aino Akté, only then to find the licence for performance refused. Happening to know Asquith, the Prime Minister, he attempted to persuade him to use his influence to get the work licensed, pointing out that the moral foundation of the British Empire was unlikely to be endangered by a few performances in German, which hardly any present would understand. Would it not be judicious to give the piece a chance? Otherwise they might run the risk of being ridiculed by the rest of the world through taking a narrow-minded attitude towards a famous work of art, as they had done so often in the past before the coming to office of Asquith's 'enlightened government'. The Prime Minister – more impressed, Beecham thought, by this last argument than any other – promised to speak to the Lord Chamberlain, and as a result some weeks later that watchdog of decency invited Sir Thomas to call on him and his second-in-command, Sir Douglas Dawson, at St James's Palace.

The two officials explained that their decision not to grant a licence had been reached as a result of the flood of letters reaching them from all over the country protesting against the stage impersonation of a sacred character, St John the Baptist. Beecham's response that *Samson et Dalila* had received a licence many years earlier, although it, too, involved biblical personages, was swiftly countered. 'There is a very great difference; in one case it is the Old Testament and in the other the New,' the Lord Chamberlain declared.

But we think we have found a way out. There is no doubt that there are many people who want to see this work and it is the view of the Prime Minister that subject to the proper safeguards we should do everything we can to enable you to give it. Now if you will consent to certain modifications of the text likely to disarm the scruples of the devout it would help us to reconsider our decision.

Beecham readily agreed to this proposal and an early conference was arranged at which, as he puts it in *A Mingled Chime: 'Salomé* would be trimmed so as to make it palatable to the taste of that large army of objectors who would never see it.' By the time all the changes were completed, St John the Baptist became Mattaniah the Prophet, and every passage between him and Salomé was deprived 'of the slightest force or meaning'. The sensual utterances of the precocious princess were refined into a longing on her part for spiritual guidance, and the celebrated line at the end of the drama, 'If you had looked upon me, you would have loved me' was transformed into 'If you had looked upon me, you would have blessed me'. The action was moved from Judea to Greece, and, says Sir Thomas, 'a lurid tale of love and revenge' became 'a comforting sermon that could have been safely preached from any country pulpit'. It was then translated into German by Alfred Kalisch.

When the rehearsals began, the Lord Chamberlain suddenly realized that, as part of the stage business, the Prophet's head would be handed to Salomé and that she would sing to it in full view of the audience for about twenty minutes. This he could not allow, so, following further discussion, it was settled that she should be given a blood-stained sword instead, but, on learning of the change, the prima donna, Aino Akté, refused to handle the weapon on the grounds that it might ruin her fine gown. Eventually the Lord Chamberlain conceded that Salomé should be presented with a large silver salver completely covered with a cloth, but that in no circumstances must any object, even the minutest, be placed underneath that might suggest by its bulging protuberance the presence of the head.

The news of all this stimulated public interest and tickets for the première fetched high prices on the black market. The Lord Chamberlain and his staff were present in a box and when the curtain rose there was a tense atmosphere on both sides of the footlights. For the first half hour the cast kept faithfully to the emasculated text, then Mme Akté forgot some of the new lines and reverted to the original German that she had sung on the Continent. The others started to follow her lead till not a phrase was used of the censored libretto. Beecham claims that his morale wilted and he saw Covent Garden, a theatre under the Lord Chamberlain's direct control, stripped of its cherished Royal Charter, himself blamed and ostracized. Then he remembered how Strauss himself, when conducting at a rehearsal of this very opera, became dissatisfied with the efforts of the singers and urged on the orchestra to drown their voices, and Sir Thomas now tried to do the same. But he realized that his tactics were doomed to eventual failure – 'for looming like a spectre before me was that dreadful final scene where the orchestral accompaniment sinks to a dynamic level that the brutalest manipulation cannot lift above a gentle *piano*, and that every word of Salomé could be heard in the last row in the gallery as she crooned away ecstatically to her empty platter'.

At the end there was tumultuous applause and several curtain calls. Then as the audience departed, Beecham was dismayed to see Lord Chamberlain and cohorts bearing down on him. His first reaction was to run, but as this might be interpreted as tacit admission of guilt he resolved to remain and face them. Then to his amazement, the Lord Chamberlain beamed at him and declared: 'It has been wonderful! We are all delighted, and I felt I could not leave without thanking you and your colleagues for the complete way in which you have met and gratified all our wishes.'

Sir Thomas comments that he never discovered whether this quite unexpected outcome was due to 'the imperfect diction of the singers, an ignorance of the language on the part of the co-editors of my text, or their diplomatic decision to put the best possible face on a dénouement that was beyond either their or my power to foresee and control'.

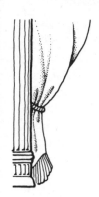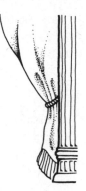

Farewells

Fun has been made in the past of the number of farewells divas give. The hardest thing a Queen of Song has to do in her life is to step down from that throne for good. The temptation is often irresistible, having moved a few steps away, to run back and sit down again before anyone else can reach it.

Giulia Grisi gave nine farewell performances in 1861. Patti started by giving one in New York in 1887, followed by six at Covent Garden, and at least twenty more during the rest of her life.

Geraldine Farrar was one of the few singers who retired when she was forty and who made her farewell truly final. During that season at the Met she appeared in turn as Marguerite, Butterfly, Louise, Manon and Carmen, and on each occasion her fans, the 'Gerryflappers', grew increasingly hysterical. 'Children,' she begged them on one occasion, 'this is no funeral.'

Then, on the very last night, she sang the title role in Leoncavallo's *Zaza*, when banners hung from the boxes, balloons floated everywhere, and after the second act she was presented with a crown and sceptre. 'I don't want a tear in this house,' she said at the final curtain. 'I am leaving because I want to go.' Backstage she shared out her costumes and props among her most long-serving 'Gerryflappers' to prove that this was indeed her swan-song and, putting on an outfit made for her by some of them, she made a regal exit from the place that, as Vincent Sheean has written, she could almost have called 'my opera house' as Melba had Covent Garden.

Melba gave the first and most famous of her many farewells at Covent Garden on 8 June 1926, when she was sixty-five and had reigned thirty-eight years.

Beverley Nichols has related how he visited her the day before and found her preparing her speech for the occasion. 'It's driving me mad!' she exclaimed. 'Look at all the people I have to thank.' He went through the notes she handed him. It read like a court circular, bringing in every monarch, royal highness, peer, ambassador, etc. she knew, then the conductors, the orchestra and the backstage staff, and lastly she had jotted down the name 'Austin'. Nichols asked who he was and she answered: 'The stage-door keeper. He's been here for forty years. And he's always seen me into my carriage.'

Nichols claims that, greatly daring, he flung the papers into the fireplace, saying: 'You can forget all that. You can curtsy to the royals and say something nice about the orchestra, but after that you need only mention Austin. In precisely the words you've just spoken.'

'I've never heard anything so ridiculous!' Melba retorted. They argued and there was quite a scene. She told him angrily that he was impossible and need not stay to lunch. But when Nichols left it was with a smile, for he felt that he had won.

Thanks to His Master's Voice Company having recorded, without Nellie's knowledge, the last half of that memorable performance, her speech has been preserved for posterity. Addressing Lord Stanley, head of the London Opera Syndicate, she said: 'I thank you for all the beautiful things you've said of me. I have so many people to thank tonight. . . . And I have to thank my dear old friend Austin, who has been at the stage door for forty years, and over those forty years for thirty-six years he has put me in my carriage and has always bid me good-night. . . . You can imagine – what I feel . . . .'

At this, says Beverley Nichols, there was a roar of applause that seemed to shake the old opera house to its foundations. 'It was the farewell to end all farewells.'

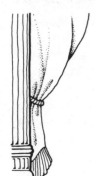
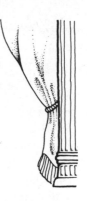

Making Retirement
Bearable

Right from the dawn of the divas few have faced retirement with equanimity. When Catherine Tofts left the stage in 1708, she became mentally deranged and, having played queens so often in opera, would order her servants to prepare her throne and attend to her on bended knees. This caused Richard Steele to write in *The Tatler*:

Greatness of soul has reduced the unhappy princess to a voluntary retirement where she now passes the time among the woods and forests thinking on the crowns and sceptres she has lost, and often humming over in her solitude: 'I was born of royal race. Yet must wander in disgrace, etc.' But for fear of being overheard, and her quality known, she usually sang it in Italian.

Last century's great Queen of Song, Adelina Patti, spent the latter part of her life in a mock-Gothic stone mansion situated in the beautiful heart of the Swansea Valley in South Wales. It was christened by her Craig-y-Nos Castle after the limestone mass, the 'Rock of Night', facing it to the west and which with appropriate discretion concealed the setting sun. She spent more than £2 million in today's values enlarging and embellishing her new home, adding a private theatre, a copy in miniature of the opera house at Bayreuth, with her monogram in gold over the proscenium arch and the names of the composers in whose works she had sung adorning the walls. There was a backdrop depicting Adelina as Semiramide driving a chariot, and also no fewer than 126 settings. To Craig-y-Nos she invited in turn all the friends who admired her most, thus maintaining the atmosphere of adulation which she craved.

Monsieur de Saxe was a nineteenth-century opera enthusiast who prided himself on never having missed a first night anywhere and to have known every artist of consequence. Blanche Marchesi in *A Singer's Pilgrimage* has recorded the description (possibly somewhat highly-coloured) he gave her of his first visit to Craig-y-Nos. After accepting an invitation, he received a second letter from Patti's secretary confiding that it was customary on such occasions for a guest to bring a large bouquet in a cardboard box similar to a hat-box. When on reaching the Castle, Saxe stepped out of the carriage a footman took the container from him. Neither the diva nor her second husband, the tenor Nicolini, were there to welcome him, and instead another footman in silk stockings led the way through a conservatory and between two rows of shrieking parrots and cockatoos, dancing wildly on their perches and lunging viciously at the new arrival. He was then conducted along a seemingly interminable gallery to his bedroom, where a valet informed him that dinner was at a certain hour when he would have to appear in the drawing-room.

Soon after the man had left, a lady's maid entered, carrying a large tray covered with jewel-boxes, and said that wishing to do a special favour to her guest, Mme Patti was giving Monsieur the privilege of choosing the jewels which she would wear that evening. The servant then spread out before him complete sets of rubies, emeralds, sapphires, diamonds and pearls, each set consisting of a tiara, a necklace, brooches, rings, earrings and bracelets. Very embarrassed, Saxe chose the ruby set, and with a curtsy the maid withdrew.

At last the dinner bell rang with startling loudness, and Saxe went to the drawing-room where he found the other guests already waiting on either side of the doorway, through which emerged a few minutes later Mme Patti in a magnificent Worth evening dress, wearing the ruby parure and leaning on Nicolini's arm, bowing right and left, holding out her hand for a kiss here, a kiss there, and eventually greeting M. de Saxe. After pointing out that she was wearing the jewels he had chosen, she smiled and passed with her husband ahead of the guests into the dining-room.

At table, several of the party seemed to know from past experience that they were expected to pay compliments to their hostess throughout the meal, and the radiance of her smile grew as the flattery became more fulsome. According to Saxe, one young woman called across the table to her sister: 'Isn't she divine to-night?' To which the reply was: 'Be quiet – there are no words to express her beauty.' And the diva responded by turning to the others and asking: 'Are they not delightful children?'

Saxe claimed that it was impossible to start a conversation about any subject except Patti, so he abandoned attempts to do so. He noticed that Nicolini drank his own special wine, whilst one of inferior vintage was served to the guests. He tasted the food put on his wife's plate, then declared solemnly every time: 'You can eat it.' The cigars offered later were also like the wine, superior for the host.

At the end of the dinner when the ladies retired into the drawing-room, Patti said: '*A tout à l'heure au théâtre.*' Then she left with a curtsy, to which the others responded as if to a queen.

Saxe was then told that there would be a performance in the Castle's theatre, where Patti would entertain them by appearing in her favourite roles. The ringing of a bell was the signal for all to seat themselves in the front stalls, and turning round Saxe saw that the back was filled with a crowd of tradesmen, farmers, villagers and servants, whom he suspected had been forced to accept invitations for business reasons.

When the curtain rose, Adelina appeared costumed as Violetta in a scene from *La traviata*, accompanied by Wilhelm Ganz at the piano. To Saxe's amazement, Alfredo was played in dumb show by the butler, as Nicolini did not feel in the mood that evening to sing. As the excerpt ended, loud applause and cheering led by the servants came from the back, and after many curtain calls artificial flowers and garlands were hurled over the guests' heads and fell at the feet of the diva, who, smiling and sending out kisses from her fingertips, bowed and pressed the floral tributes to her heart. Then, when the curtain was brought down for the last time, footmen carrying a huge basket came on to the stage and picked up all the flowers, putting them carefully away to be used again the next night.

According to Blanche Marchesi, another friend of hers was a

guest at Craig-y-Nos when, owing to a cold, Patti could not sing, so told the house party that rather than disappoint them she would do the next best thing. This was to appear on the stage in a gondola festooned with flowers, which was propelled to and fro, receiving at each reappearance frenzied applause from the claque of retainers at the rear of the auditorium.

So that they might enjoy the charms of nature, M. de Saxe and the other guests were informed next morning that they would be taken fishing with M. Nicolini, and at the appointed time a brake conveyed them to a river bank. Nobody was invited to fish but all were asked to watch their host at his favourite pastime, which politeness forced them to do in bored silence for over two hours before returning to the Castle.

Luigi Arditi, Mapleson's chief conductor and an old friend of Patti's, paints a more favourable picture of a visit to Craig-y-Nos which he made with his wife Virginia. He recalls in his memoirs that Adelina and Nicolini received them on arrival 'with open arms', and that, too tired to dress, they 'adjourned to a perfect dinner, served in a magnificent conservatory (a sort of hall of enchantment, illuminated by myriads of electric fairy lights)'. It was in fact one of the first houses to have electric light installed in it. Then, after the meal, they played billiards and listened to 'the wonderful organ which hails from Switzerland and gives a rendering of fifty or more operas, to say nothing of concerted pieces and other music'. This was an orchestrion, an elaborate sort of barrel-organ giving an orchestra-like effect. Arditi ends his account: 'I have no idea how many parures of brilliants, rubies, sapphires, pearls, emeralds, and turquoises, etc., the Diva possesses, for night after night she appears before us adorned by new splendours.'

Finale

But such worldly splendour cannot be enjoyed for ever.
The day must come when a diva makes that truly final
farewell. How appropriate it would have been in Patti's
case if her favourite parrot, Nicolini's pupil, had escaped
from the conservatory at Craig-y-Nos, and alighting on the
shoulder of some aged
impresario tottering after
her bier, had croaked
vainly into his hearing
aid: 'Cash – cash!'

Acknowledgements

Thanks are due to the following for permission to quote from the works mentioned:

The Birmingham Post and Times Newspapers Ltd. for reviews by Ernest Newman; *Opera News* for 'Applause' by George R. Marek and John Mautner's interview with Maria Jeritza; *The Musical Times* for various extracts; the authors for *Massenet* by James Harding (Dent, London) and *Red Plush and Black Velvet* by Joseph Wechsberg (Little, Brown, Boston); Hamish Hamilton Ltd., London, for *Am I Too Loud?* by Gerald Moore; The Society of Authors on behalf of the Bernard Shaw Estate for *London Music in 1888–9* (Constable) and *Music in London, 1890–1* (Constable).

PICTURE ACKNOWLEDGEMENTS

The author and publishers wish to thank the following for permission to reproduce illustrations:

Dobson Books Ltd, *The Hoffnung Music Festival* (1956), pages 98 and 106; Mary Evans Picture Library, page 157; George G. Harrap & Co Ltd, *Caught In The Act* (1976) with illustrations by Nerman, pages 26 (Birgit Nilsson) and 48 (Nellie Melba); Vivian Liff, pages 66 (Geraldine Farrar), 140 (Florencio Constantino); Punch Picture Library, pages 18, 23, 31, 59 and 129; Syndication International, page 80; *The Times*, page 83.

Note The illustration on page 41 shows Giulio Gatti-Casazza addressing singers at the Metropolitan.